A.S.A. MONOGRAPHS

General Editor: MICHAEL BANTON

5

The Structural Study of
Myth and Totemism

A.S.A. MONOGRAPHS

Published under the auspices of the Association of Social
Anthropologists of the Commonwealth

General Editor: Michael Banton

Michael Banton, editor
1. *The Relevance of Models for Social Anthropology*
2. *Political Systems and the Distribution of Power*
3. *Anthropological Approaches to the Study of Religion*
4. *The Social Anthropology of Complex Societies*

Edmund Leach, editor
5. *The Structural Study of Myth and Totemism*

Raymond Firth, editor
6. *Themes in Economic Anthropology*

I. M. Lewis, editor
7. *History and Social Anthropology*

Philip Mayer, editor
8. *Socialization: the Approach from Social Anthropology*

Mary Douglas, editor
9. *Witchcraft Confessions and Accusations*

Edwin Ardener, editor
10. *Social Anthropology and Language*

Rodney Needham, editor
11. *Rethinking Kinship and Marriage*

Abner Cohen, editor
12. *Urban Ethnicity*

THE STRUCTURAL STUDY
OF MYTH AND TOTEMISM

Edited by Edmund Leach

TAVISTOCK PUBLICATIONS

First published in 1967
by Tavistock Publications Limited
11 New Fetter Lane, London EC4

First published as a Social Science Paperback in 1968
Reprinted six times
Reprinted 1988
ISBN 0 422 72530 7

Printed in Great Britain by photolithography by
Billing & Sons Limited, Guildford, London and Worcester

This volume derives from material presented at a Conference on 'New Approaches in Social Anthropology' sponsored by the Association of Social Anthropologists of the Commonwealth, held at Jesus College, Cambridge, 24–30 June 1963

Distributed in the U.S.A. by
HARPER & ROW PUBLISHERS INC.
BARNES & NOBLE IMPORT DIVISION

Contents

Edmund Leach

Introduction

Publishers of potentially libellous novels sometimes try to save their skins by an opening assertion that 'All the characters in this book are entirely imaginary'. Much the same might be said of the leading off-stage character in this set of critical essays: each of the authors has his own fixed ideas about the nature of Lévi-Strauss's thought and is prepared to do battle on ground of his own choosing. But the different Lévi-Strauss figures which are thus turned into Aunt Sally do not seem to me to share a great deal in common; just where they connect up with the living Lévi-Strauss, Professor at the Collège de France, is not for me to say. If this book provides illumination it will be because of the light it throws upon the assumptions and attitudes of particular British social anthropologists rather than because of any consistent analysis of the work of Continental Europe's most distinguished living anthropologist.

The symposium originated in the spring of 1963, when members of the Association of Social Anthropologists meeting at Oxford decided to devote a future session to a series of papers concerning the work of Lévi-Strauss. By the time that I myself was brought into the matter as seminar convener, the principal contributors had already agreed to prepare papers. At that stage I saw my role as strictly catalytic and I circulated to participants copies of an English translation of 'La Geste d'Asdiwal' which had been prepared for me by Mr Nicholas Mann. I am particularly grateful to Professor Lévi-Strauss and Mr Mann for allowing this translation to appear as the headpiece of these printed proceedings.

I should here explain that Dr Douglas's contribution was prepared for an audience which did not have immediate access to the Lévi-Strauss essay and on that account her paper includes a précis of the document which she is criticizing. This means

---

that pp. 53-60 of this book to some extent repeat what has already appeared at pp. 1-47. But Dr Douglas's précis is itself an integral part of her analysis and a comparison between the original and the précis may be of some interest in itself.

It was originally intended that the seminar should take place in January 1964 and drafts of four of the papers printed here were actually prepared by that date. However, as things turned out, the meeting was not held until June 1964. The proceedings fell into three parts. The first session, with the general title 'Method in the Analysis of Myth', was focused around papers by Dr Douglas and Dr Burridge; the second, entitled 'General and Particular Views of Totemism', developed out of a paper by Dr Mendelson and a more or less off-the-cuff contribution from Professor Worsley. The final session had as theme 'The Significance of Anthropological Studies of Myth and Totemism for other Fields of Study'. The principal paper here was one by Dr Fox, while I myself endeavoured to sum up the whole proceedings. There was a large attendance of members of the Association of Social Anthropologists, and the discussion at all three sessions (which was unrecorded) was very lively. Especially valuable contributions were made by Professor Firth, Dr Freeman, and Dr Yalman.

The various contributors have all reworked their original papers and the texts printed here are in some cases substantially different from the originals. This applies especially to the contributions by Burridge and Worsley. In these printed proceedings a review of Lévi-Strauss's *Le Cru et le cuit* by Dr Yalman has been inserted immediately after Dr Douglas's paper, but the reader should bear in mind that this book had not been published at the date of the original symposium. If it had appeared earlier the seminar papers and discussions might have taken rather a different line. For example, Dr Douglas expresses surprise and puzzlement that Lévi-Strauss should insist that myth is wholly unlike poetry because 'poetry is a kind of speech which cannot be translated except at the cost of serious distortions; whereas the mythical value of myths remains preserved through the worst translation'. Dr Douglas seems to think that this argument must be invalid because Lévi-Strauss has himself made a structural analysis of a poem by Baudelaire using procedures similar to those by which he analyses the structure of myths. There is clearly a misunderstanding here. Dr Douglas might have grasped Lévi-Strauss's meaning more easily if she had read *Le Cru et le cuit*, where it is argued in very explicit terms that the mode by which myths convey meaning (or, rather, experience) is similar to the mode by which music conveys experience. Lévi-Strauss seems to claim that we respond to the patterned structures of myth in much the same way as we respond to the repetitions of counterpoint and to the combinations of harmony. On this analogy the details of particular mythical stories are like the melody of a particular musical phrase, and melody is a relatively trivial element in the communication that is achieved when we listen to music. In contrast, in poetry, the actual meaning of the words is always of primary significance.

But although I feel that Dr Douglas's criticism is unjustified on this particular point, there are other parts of her essay with which I feel much sympathy. She notes, for example, that Lévi-Strauss claims that anyone can recognize the mythic quality of myth and she draws attention to Ricoeur's comment that Lévi-Strauss's 'examples of mythic thought have been taken from the geographical areas of totemism and never from Semitic, pre-Hellenic, or Indo-European areas'. This is an important point. Virtually the only myths which Lévi-Strauss considers are those in which some or all of the characters in the story are animals endowed with human attributes. This delimitation makes it particularly easy for Lévi-Strauss to support Rousseau's thesis that a distinction between Humanity and Animality, or between Culture and Nature, is one of the primary preoccupations of primitive human thought. Those of us who approach the problem of mythical interpretation in rather a different way often find that the question 'What is myth, what is not myth?' can be an extremely difficult one. It was the Greeks who first began to make a distinction between myth and history, but they made it in a hesitant way and it is still very much open to doubt whether the distinctions which they and their successors have made are really satisfactory. Since arbitrariness of the content of verbal categories is a major theme in Lévi-Strauss's writing concerning *La Pensée sauvage*,

Edmund Leach

I find it surprising that he should seem so certain that myth is a *natural* category!

On the other hand, I find myself quite out of sympathy with Dr Douglas when, in her last few paragraphs, she attacks Lévi-Strauss's image that man the maker of culture is like a *bricoleur*, building up his collective representations out of the bric-à-brac residues of history and the oddments of the physical environment. Unlike Dr Douglas, I can see in this regard no fundamental difference between the 'culture of the Old Testament' and that of the Australian aborigines.

Although I am personally more closely addicted to Lévi-Strauss's methods than are most of my colleagues as represented in this book, I certainly would not contend that Lévi-Strauss's techniques for the analysis of myth and totemism are the only techniques that can usefully be followed, and I am certain that Lévi-Strauss himself would never dream of suggesting any such thing. The road to analytical progress is not through the slavish imitation of established procedures, be they those of Lévi-Strauss or anyone else. We will only break new ground when we systematically try out modifications or even inversions of previously formulated argument. In this respect Dr Burridge's paper seems to me to fall into two roughly equal halves. The first part is mainly concerned with a demonstration of the importance of Hegelian categories in Lévi-Strauss's thinking. The second, which I myself find the more stimulating, is mainly concerned with the analysis of a myth which Dr Burridge himself recorded in the field. Dr Burridge claims that his analytical procedure is one which 'climbs blatantly on Lévi-Strauss's broad back but goes to content rather than to form'. The interpretation which results is clearly not one which Lévi-Strauss would have made himself, but it could not have been made at all with Lévi-Strauss's pioneering studies.

I think that the answer to the kind of criticism which Dr Burridge raises at the end of his essay is again to be found in the analogy of music. Dr Burridge complains that in Lévi-Strauss's hands 'all myths become much the same, dealing with the same things in the same way'. Just how far this is true will depend upon the level at which the analysis is being made. There is, for example, clearly a sense in which communication through music is 'all of the same kind' in contrast, that is, with other forms of communication such as that through verbal speech. Similarly, in linguistics, there are universals which are true of all languages, e.g. binary oppositions between distinctive features. Yet it is possible to say a great variety of things both in music and in common speech. It is true that at one level Lévi-Strauss *is* concerned to distinguish for us the common language of myth in a sense analogous to that with which we might speak of the common language of music. But I feel bound to ask how Dr Burridge can be so sure that this 'uniformity' is 'spurious'?

In any case, this is not the only level at which Lévi-Strauss's analysis operates. Dr Mendelson's essay is primarily a critical review of Lévi-Strauss's book *Le Totémisme aujourd'hui*. Unlike the two preceding authors, he is more concerned to explain what Lévi-Strauss's ideas are than to attack them, but he does draw attention to a difficulty which worries nearly all English readers. Lévi-Strauss covers gigantic areas of ethnographic space in a very limited number of words. It often appears, therefore, that he selects his facts and makes intuitive judgements in a very arbitrary way. The Englishman with his empiricist bias is always likely to feel haunted by the question 'Yes, this is all very well, but what if *all* the facts (or only *different* facts) were taken into account?'

And this I think is why Professor Worsley's paper is so extremely valuable.

So far as this symposium is concerned, Professor Worsley has two major merits. One is that he shares with Lévi-Strauss a Marxist or near Marxist orientation so that he has a sympathetic understanding for the way in which Lévi-Strauss handles his materials. At the same time he is keenly aware of the distinction between the French love of logical order and the English love of empirical detail. Finally, he has the great advantage over all the other contributors that he has himself carried out detailed fieldwork among an Australian aboriginal group in which totemism is still of major significance in social affairs. Worsley's paper is really the pivot of the book and needs to be read very carefully. It shows up very well both the merits and the limitations of Lévi-Strauss's type of analysis for the interpretation of a body of empirical ethnographic material. But besides this, the new concepts which he introduces as a borrowing from the language psychologist Vygotsky deserve our close attention.

Lévi-Strauss's *La Pensée sauvage* is a *tour de force* which seems to achieve the impossible by demonstrating that logical order can be found even among the most intractable ethnographic materials. Yet, of course, all of us who are anthropologists are convinced that *some* such order can be found. We would not be doing our job at all unless we thought that ethnographic materials made sense. But what kind of sense? In *La Pensée sauvage* the categories of totemism and the categories of taxonomic systems are hardly distinguished. But Worsley, following Vygotsky, suggests that in primitive thought there may be several different *kinds* of classification of different degrees of distinctiveness, which he proposes to label 'congeries', 'complex', and 'concept'. Here is an idea which deserves close attention and much further elaboration.

At the same time I should make clear that I personally do not go all the way with Professor Worsley in his scepticism. For example, he seems to me clearly at fault in supposing that gender in French equates with sex and that *on that account* it is palpably absurd to think that there is 'some inner conceptual and social meaning to the French classification of all things into masculine and feminine'. Gender does *not* equate with sex; sex is one of the 'things' which is classified by gender. It is precisely because Englishmen habitually make this kind of mistake that they find difficulty in following such reasoning as that of Lévi-Strauss.

And here I think is a point on which the various contributors to this book (other than myself and perhaps Dr Yalman) are in approximate agreement. They are not trying to argue that Lévi-Strauss is wrong but that he somehow gives the impression that the problem is too easy. They complain that Lévi-Strauss tries to reduce all ethnographic materials to one kind. Is there not more to it than just binary discrimination? In some respects I think the critics miss the point and yet they have a case. It is certainly evident that *some* mental processes are somewhat similar to those of a digital computer. But if we go on from here to say that 'the human brain is like a computer mechanism' we need to understand that the computer in question is of a complexity undreamed of by electronic engineers. Not only does the human brain combine attributes of digital and analogue computers but the discriminating principles are multidimensional on a grand scale. Where an electronic computer has just two connections, one positive and one negative, to make a binary flip-flop, the human mechanism seems to be wired up with enormous varieties of redundancy, one hundred or more connections at a time. The messages that emerge from such an apparatus are hardly likely to be amenable to *simple* logical analysis. Worsley's point is that a satisfactory interpretation may require us to think of several different kinds of logic operating at the same time. In this connection I may quote a field report from a pupil of mine, Mr Geoffrey Benjamin, who has been working among the Temiar-Senoi in the Malaysian jungle:

'You asked tentatively some months ago whether I'd got anything on what the Temiar think of animals – I've now got more than I can handle (taxonomically, that is). Lévi-Strauss would jump for joy – there is no animal species, from grubs to tigers, to which they are neutral. Every species I've encountered so far is categorized somewhere in a very complex system of pigeonholes. And furthermore many plants fit into the same holes. Some of the categories are species that cause convulsions if eaten, species that one must not tame, species one must share around as meat, species that must not be laughed at (mainly invertebrates), species that have a whole series of avoidance names, species everyone may eat, species that only people in the following (partially inclusive) social categories may eat – children, women, parents of young children, old men, old women – species that only certain individuals dare eat, and so on. And to back it up the full cycle of myths is coming out. Most are relatable to the central creation myth . . . the creator seems to be Mt Changhai in Perak! The Mt Changhai has a series of animal familiars who each carry out an allotted task, and most of whom are relatable to a definite species of tree, all of which is relevant

to present-day practices. The other thing is that the other
Aboriginal tribes, Semai, Lanop, Bateq, etc. play a co-
ordinate part in these concepts and it begins to look as if
they are the "clans" of a very thorough-going totemism.'

I cannot help feeling that empirical material of this kind of
complexity may be more amenable to analysis on the lines
Worsley suggests than by the relatively simple binary analysis
suggested by Lévi-Strauss.

Dr Fox's paper is the joker in the pack, but in some ways it
is the one which is most likely to lead to controversial discussion.
The other papers take as their starting-point the recent work of
Lévi-Strauss; Dr Fox goes back to Freud's classic *Totem and
Taboo.*

At a factual level he shows a number of interesting things. In
the first place what Freud actually said is substantially different
from what a number of his anthropological critics have thought
that he said! It is certainly a surprise to me to learn that his
incest theory was tied in with a theory about unilineal descent.
Freud's views were firmly based in evolutionist assumptions,
but, allowing for that, his arguments seem to fit quite well with
recent sociological diagnosis of the relations between incest
attitudes and descent rules.

Dr Fox shows that 'both Freud and Lévi-Strauss are basically
interested in the same question; how did *Homo* come to be
sapiens? What sets man off from Nature while leaving him part
of Nature?' But he goes on to make a kind of binary distinction
in which he claims that 'for Freud the break-through is an
affective phenomenon: for Lévi-Strauss it is intellectual'. And
the author's aim, it seems, is to attack Lévi-Strauss for his
excessively intellectualist sociological approach in contrast to
the view that 'neither the feelings nor the institutions should
be taken for granted but we must seek for an interaction
between them'. Dr Fox emphasizes the 'feedback' between
individual psychology and sociological fact and seems to think
that Lévi-Strauss leaves this out. I myself find this a rather
curious view, for 'feedback' is a concept of which Lévi-Strauss
has an extremely sophisticated understanding and the conclusion of *Le Cru et le cuit*, though almost too metaphysical to

permit translation, is concerned precisely with the feedback between culture and thought, as manifested in myth. Let me quote:

'Les mythes signifient l'esprit, qui les élabore au moyen de monde dont il fait lui-même partie. Ainsi peuvent être simultanément engendrés, les mythes eux-mêmes par l'esprit qui les cause, et par les mythes, une image du monde déjà inscrite dans l'architecture de l'esprit' (Lévi-Strauss, 1964, p. 346).

If Dr Fox can achieve the feat of translating this curious form of words into his own language code he will see that Lévi-Strauss is saying that myth forms the bridge between emotive experience and intellectualist thought which Dr Fox himself thinks is so important, and he is also saying something rather profound about the way in which myth is perpetuated, a problem which, on Dr Fox's analysis, was central to Freud's psychosocial theory, but which Freud 'solved' only by resort to crude Lamarckian presuppositions.

From these comments on the finished essays of my fellow contributors, it will be apparent that in my role of convener of the A.S.A. meeting I found myself in a somewhat paradoxical position. I do not consider that I am a slavish imitator of Lévi-Strauss but, as is plainly apparent from my essay collection *Rethinking Anthropology* (Leach, 1961), I have been greatly influenced by Lévi-Strauss's work. My fellow contributors are less directly in his debt, and many of those who attended the A.S.A. meeting and contributed to the discussion did not appear to have read Lévi-Strauss's work at all. Thus while some of the criticisms raised were genuinely felt and derived from the basically different points of view of the English empiricist and the French intellectual, others seemed to depend either on English arrogance or straight misinformation. Some commentators for example, secure in their certainty of the merits of orthodox British social anthropology, wanted to dismiss the current enthusiasm for Lévi-Strauss as just 'a passing fashion', but of course everything is a passing fashion. Malinowski's critics raised the same argument forty years ago and of course they were right. We no longer adhere to the doctrines which Malinowski espoused with such enthusiasm. Nevertheless, anthropology today would be a wholly different thing if Malinowski had never existed. Lévi-Strauss is important in this same sense. Whatever may have become of his theories in thirty years' time he will certainly have left a lasting mark upon our subject. At the same time, there is a sense in which Lévi-Strauss's views *are* a fashion; and I think we can under- stand why. Functionalism in anthropology, especially in the form espoused by Malinowski, proved a constrictive doctrine, for if everything must be seen in context how can one generalize at all? Lévi-Strauss's 'structuralism' is the dialectical reaction to 'functionalism' in this narrow sense. At the very least it is to Lévi-Strauss's lasting credit that he has made it once again intellectually respectable to indulge in broad cross-cultural comparisons, especially in areas where sophisticated anthro- pologists have been evading comparison ever since the days of Sir James Frazer.

All the same it is worth emphasizing that, although Lévi- Strauss's contribution represents a radical innovation so far as social anthropology is concerned, his arguments have a respect- able ancestry in other disciplines. Vladimir Propp's study of the folktale was originally published as far back as 1928 (Propp, 1958; Lévi-Strauss, 1960); Georges Dumézil's detailed studies of Indo-European mythology date back at least to 1929 (Dumézil, 1940, preface), and both these authors stand very close to Lévi-Strauss. What Lévi-Strauss has really done is to draw on the notion of 'structure' employed by linguists, folk- lorists, certain psycho-analysts, mathematicians, and com- munication engineers, and apply this analytical concept to the categories of orthodox ethnography. This process has proved disturbing to the British social anthropologists only because they themselves had formulated a rather different, biologically based, notion of structure, so that they have sometimes tended to write as if Lévi-Strauss were infringing British patents!

Many English anthropologists are also put off by what may be called the oracular elegance of much that Lévi-Strauss writes. From this side of the Channel it seems to be a very general failing of French intellectuals that they are liable to wrap up profundity in verbal obscurity. Some passages of Lévi-Strauss when translated into English seem almost meaningless. Yet to believe that the only things worth saying are those which can be writ plain in the English language seems to me a very arrogant assumption. Lévi-Strauss often manages to give me ideas even when I don't really know what he is saying.

My fellow contributors have naturally emphasized the points where Lévi-Strauss seems to diverge from other more familiar anthropologists. But it would be a mistake to think that Lévi-Strauss is trying to be heretical on all fronts at once. For example, so far as myth analysis is concerned, he largely accepts Malinowski's view that, in any particular cultural context, 'myth is a charter for social action'. But in addition he is interested in further problems which Malinowski scarcely considered. For example, questions of the following kinds necessarily entail cross-cultural inquiry. (1) Is the manner in which myths are constructed and in which they convey their messages similar in all cultural situations or is it not? (2) Are there some mythical themes which are universals or nearly so and which can therefore be studied cross-culturally as well as in their particular cultural contexts? In so far as the answer to the second of these questions is 'Yes', it is obvious that there are very few such themes. Lévi-Strauss is not saying that *all* myths belong to this very limited category but only that myths of this limited category are the ones which are specially interesting from a cross-cultural point of view. Examples of universal myth problems are: Is death final? Is an incest rule necessary? How did humanity begin? Such problems are not only universal, they are quite fundamental, and I was astonished to find that some contributors to the seminar discussion actually referred to these themes as 'quite trivial'!

It is a misrepresentation to suggest that Lévi-Strauss is saying that 'all myths are the same'. He is arguing rather that, at a certain level of abstraction, the dialectical redundant structure of all myths is the same, or perhaps one should say, 'constitutes a set of variations on a common theme'. Some of the seminar discussants, including perhaps Dr Douglas, seemed to think that Lévi-Strauss's demonstrations of structural similarity amount to no more than demonstrations of Lévi-Strauss's own ingenuity. But here I must disagree. If we accept

Lévi-Strauss's own analogy that there is a language of myth, then this language presents us with problems similar to those of decoding a completely unknown prehistoric script such as, for example, the celebrated Cretan Linear B. The cryptographic procedures for decoding such a language are well understood. They are structural. When such a language is finally decoded the first attempts at translation are likely to be greeted with derision. But as more and more texts fall into the same pattern everyone must finally accept the truth. Scholars all now agree that Linear B is a form of ancient Greek, despite the fact that the original suggestion that this might be so was thought quite absurd. In the same way, it seems to me that anthropologists had good grounds for being thoroughly sceptical about Lévi-Strauss's 'structural analysis of myth' when this technique was first expounded in 1955, but that since the publication of *Le Cru et le cuit* in the autumn of 1964 it is possible to quibble only about details. Lévi-Strauss has shown that there *is* such a thing as 'a language of myth', and he has shown what sort of language it is and how it conveys significance.

From my own point of view he has done much more than that. He has provided us with a new set of hypotheses about familiar materials. We can look again at what we thought was understood and begin to gain entirely new insights. It is not a question of Lévi-Strauss being right or Lévi-Strauss being wrong; it is more like literary or dramatic criticism. Faced with the challenge of a new point of view one is suddenly able to see the familiar in quite a different way and to understand something which was previously invisible.

On the matter of totemism I have already expressed elsewhere (Leach, 1964) my admiration, my doubts, and my qualifications of Lévi-Strauss's analysis, and I do not want to add further to what is said by other contributors to this book on this particular theme. But it does seem to me worth emphasizing that, besides the Hegelian-Marxist element which keeps on turning up in Lévi-Strauss's arguments, there is also an Existentialist background, which is relevant in a number of different ways. It is relevant to the thesis that the order which we perceive in the world is something which we impose upon it and that man has choice to order the world in different ways in a quite arbitrary

manner – the *bricoleur* of *La Pensée sauvage*; and it is relevant
also to the theme that structures of relationship are subject to
transformation.

At the end of *Tristes Tropiques* Lévi-Strauss argues that we
cannot choose to be alone, it must be 'we' or 'nothing'. But in
choosing 'we' there is an almost infinite choice as to what kind
of 'we' it shall be. Myth is part of the apparatus through which
we make that choice clear to ourselves and so is totemism, but
the choice itself is free, not determined. We can choose how
we are related to one another or to our environment or even
to that enigmatic Lévi-Straussian cat whose totemic Sphinx-
like qualities have fascinated both Dr Burridge and Dr
Mendelson.

REFERENCES

DUMÉZIL, G. 1940. *Mitra Varuna: Essai sur deux représentations indo-européennes de la souveranité* (Bibliothèque de l'École des Hautes Études: Sciences Religieuses, Vol. 56). Paris.

LEACH, E. R. 1961. *Rethinking Anthropology*. London: Athlone Press.

—— 1964. Telstar et les aborigènes ou 'La Pensée sauvage'. *Annales* No. 6, Nov.-Dec. Paris.

LÉVI-STRAUSS, C. 1958. La Geste d'Asdiwal (*École Pratique des Hautes Études, Section des Sciences Religieuses*. Extr. Annuaire 1958-1959, pp. 3-43). Reprinted in *Les Temps modernes*, March 1961.

—— 1960. La Structure et la Forme. Réflexions sur un ouvrage de Vladimir Propp. *Cahiers de l'Institut de Science Économique Appliquée* (Paris) No. 99. March (Série M. No. 7), pp. 3-36.

—— 1962a. *Le Totémisme aujourd'hui* (English translation, 1964a. *Totemism*. London: Merlin Press).

—— 1962b. *La Pensée sauvage*. Paris: Plon.

—— 1964. *Mythologiques: Le Cru et le cuit*. Paris: Plon.

PROPP, V. 1958. Morphology of the Folk Tale (English translation from the Russian) Part III. *International Journal of American Linguistics* 24: 4.

VYGOTSKY, L. S. 1962. *Thought and Language* (edited & translated by E. Hanfmann & G. Vankar) (Studies in Communication). Cambridge, Mass: M.I.T. Press.

PART I

The Structural Study of Myth

Claude Lévi-Strauss

The Story of Asdiwal

*Since 1963 Lévi-Strauss and his associates have published
a variety of 'structural analyses' of myth, but prior to the
appearance of* Le Cru et le cuit *in the autumn of 1964
'La Geste d'Asdiwal' was, by general consent, the most
successful of all these pieces. 'Asdiwal' has twice appeared
in French, but this is the first English translation. The
Editor is deeply indebted to Professor Lévi-Strauss for
granting permission to publish the translation and to Mr
Nicholas Mann for making it.*

I

This study of a native myth from the Pacific coast of Canada
has two aims. First, to isolate and compare the *various levels*
on which the myth evolves: geographic, economic, sociological,
and cosmological – each one of these levels, together with the
symbolism proper to it, being seen as a transformation of an
underlying logical structure common to all of them. And, second,
to compare the *different versions* of the myth and to look for the
meaning of the discrepancies between them, or between some
of them; for, since they all come from the same people (but are
recorded in different parts of their territory), these variations
cannot be explained in terms of dissimilar beliefs, languages, or
institutions.

The story of Asdiwal, which comes from the Tsimshian
Indians, is known to us in four versions, collected some sixty
years ago by Franz Boas (1895; 1902; 1912; 1916).

We shall begin by calling attention to certain facts which
must be known if the myth is to be understood.

The Tsimshian Indians, with the Tlingit and the Haida,
belong to the northern group of cultures on the Northwest
Pacific coast. They live in British Columbia, immediately south
of Alaska, in a region which embraces the basins of the Nass
and Skeena Rivers, the coastal region stretching between their

1

estuaries, and, further inland, the land drained by the two rivers and their tributaries. The Nass in the North and the Skeena in the south both flow in a northeast-southwesterly direction, and are approximately parallel. The Nass, however, is slightly nearer North-South in orientation, a detail which, as we shall see, is not entirely devoid of importance.

This territory was divided between three local groups, distinguished by their different dialects: in the upper reaches of the Skeena, the Gitskan; in the lower reaches and the coastal region, the Tsimshian themselves; and in the valleys of the Nass and its tributaries, the Nisqa. Three of the versions of the myth of Asdiwal were recorded on the coast and in Tsimshian dialect (Boas, 1895, pp. 285-288; 1912, pp. 71-146; 1916, pp. 243-245 and the comparative analysis, pp. 792-824), the fourth at the mouth of the Nass, in Nisqa dialect (Boas, 1902, pp. 225-228). It is this last which, when compared with the other three, reveals the most marked differences.

Like all the peoples on the Northwest Pacific Coast, the Tsimshian had no agriculture. During the summer, the women's work was to collect fruit, berries, plants, and wild roots, while the men hunted bears and goats in the mountains and seals and sea-lions on the coastal reefs. They also practised deep-sea fishery, catching mainly cod and halibut, but also herring nearer the shore. It was, however, the complex rhythm of river-fishing that made the deepest impression upon the life of the tribe. Whereas the Nisqa were relatively settled, the Tsimshian moved, according to the seasons, between their winter villages, which were situated in the coastal region, and their fishing-places, either on the Nass or the Skeena.

At the end of the winter, when stores of smoked fish, dried meat, fat, and preserved fruits were running low, or were even completely exhausted, the natives would undergo periods of severe famine, an echo of which is found in the myth. At such times they anxiously awaited the arrival of the candlefish[1] which would go up the Nass (which was still frozen to start with) for a period of about six weeks in order to spawn (Goddard, 1934, p. 68). This would begin about 1 March, and the entire Skeena population would travel along the coast in boats as far as the Nass in order to take up position on the fishing-grounds, which were family properties. The period from 15 February to 15 March was called, not without reason, the 'Month when Candlefish is Eaten' and that which followed, from 15 March to 15 April, the 'Month when Candlefish is Cooked' (to extract its oil). This operation was strictly taboo to men, whereas the women were obliged to use their naked breasts to press the fish; the oil-cake residue had to be left to become rotten from maggots and putrefaction and, despite the pestilential stench, it had to be left in the immediate vicinity of the dwelling-houses until the work was finished (Boas, 1916, pp. 398-399 and 44-45).

Then everyone would return by the same route to the Skeena for the second major event, which was the arrival of the salmon fished in June and July (the 'Salmon Months'). Once the fish was smoked and stored away for the year, the families would go up to the mountains, where the men would hunt while the women laid up stocks of fruit and berries. With the coming of the frost in the ritual 'Month of the Spinning Tops' (which were spun on the ice), people settled down in permanent villages for the winter. During this period the men used sometimes to go off hunting again for a few days or a few weeks. Finally, towards 15 November, came the 'Taboo Month', which marked the inauguration of the great winter ceremonies, in preparation for which the men were subjected to various restrictions.

Let us remember, too, that the Tsimshian were divided into four non-localized matrilineal clans, which were strictly exogamous and divided into lineages, descent lines, and households: the Eagles, the Ravens, the Wolves, and the Bears, also, that the permanent villages were the seat of chiefdoms (generally called 'tribes' by native informants); and finally that Tsimshian society was divided into (three) hereditary castes with bilateral inheritance of caste status (each individual was supposed to marry according to his rank): the 'Real People' or reigning familes, the 'Nobles', and the 'People', which last comprised all those who (failing a purchase of rank by generous potlatches) were unable to assert an equal degree of nobility in both lines of their descent (Boas 1916, pp. 478-514; Garfield, 1939, pp. 173-174 and 177-178; Garfield, Wingert & Barbeau, 1951, pp. 1-34).

II

Now follows a summary of the story of Asdiwal taken from Boas (1912) which will serve as a point of reference. This version was recorded on the coast at Port Simpson in Tsimshian dialect. Boas published the native text together with an English translation.

Famine reigns in the Skeena valley; the river is frozen and it is winter. A mother and her daughter, both of whose husbands have died of hunger, both remember independently the happy times when they lived together and there was no dearth of food. Released by the death of their husbands, they simultaneously decide to meet and set off at the same moment. Since the mother lives down-river and the daughter up-river, the former goes eastwards and the latter westwards. They both travel on the frozen bed of the Skeena and meet half-way.

Weeping with hunger and sorrow, the two women pitch camp on the bank at the foot of a tree, not far from which they find, poor pittance that it is, a rotten berry, which they sadly share.

During the night, a stranger visits the young widow. It is soon learned that his name is Hatsenas,[2] a term which means, in Tsimshian, a bird of good omen. Thanks to him, the women start to find food regularly, and the younger of the two becomes the wife of their mysterious protector and soon gives birth to a son, Asdiwal (Asiwa, Boas, 1895; Asi-hwil, Boas, 1902).[3] His father speeds up his growth by supernatural means and gives him various magic objects: a bow and arrows which never miss for hunting, a quiver, a lance, a basket, snow-shoes, a bark raincoat, and a hat, all of which will enable the hero to overcome all obstacles, make himself invisible, and procure an inexhaustible supply of food. Hatsenas then disappears and the elder of the two women dies.

Asdiwal and his mother pursue their course westwards and settle down in her native village, Gitsalasert, in the Skeena Canyon (Boas, 1912, p. 83). One day a white she-bear comes down the valley.

Hunted by Asdiwal, who almost catches it thanks to his

magic objects, the bear starts to climb up a vertical ladder. Asdiwal follows it up to the heavens, which he sees as a vast prairie, covered with grass and all kinds of flowers. The bear lures him into the home of its father, the sun, and reveals itself to be a beautiful girl, Evening-Star. The marriage takes place, though not before the Sun has submitted Asdiwal to a series of trials, to which all previous suitors had succumbed (hunting wild goat in mountains which are rent by earthquakes; drawing water from a spring in a cave whose walls close in on each other; collecting wood from a tree which crushes those who try to cut it down; a period in a fiery furnace). But Asdiwal overcomes them all thanks to his magic objects and the timely intervention of his father. Won over by his son-in-law's talents, the Sun finally approves of him.

Asdiwal, however, pines for his mother. The Sun agrees to allow him to go down to earth again with his wife, and gives them, as provisions for the journey, four baskets filled with inexhaustible supplies of food, which earn the couple a grateful welcome from the villagers, who are in the midst of their winter famine.

In spite of repeated warnings from his wife, Asdiwal deceives her with a woman from his village. Evening-Star, offended, departs, followed by her tearful husband. Half-way up to heaven, Asdiwal is struck down by a look from his wife, who disappears. He dies, but is at once regretted and is brought back to life by his celestial father-in-law.

For a time, all goes well; then, once again, Asdiwal feels a twinge of nostalgia for earth. His wife agrees to accompany him as far as the earth, and there bids him a final farewell. Returning to his village, the hero learns of his mother's death. Nothing remains to hold him back, and he sets off again on his journey downstream.

When he reaches the Tsimshian village of Ginaxangioget, he seduces and marries the daughter of the local chief. To start with, the marriage is a happy one, and Asdiwal joins his four brothers-in-law on wild goat hunts, which, thanks to his magic objects, are crowned with success. When spring approaches, the whole family moves house, staying first at Metlakatla, and then setting off by boat for the river Nass, going up along the coast. A head wind forces them to a halt and they camp for a while at Ksemaksén. There, things go wrong because of a dispute between Asdiwal and his brothers-in-law over the respective merits of mountain-hunters and sea-hunters. A competition takes place – Asdiwal returns from the mountains with four bears that he has killed, while the brothers-in-law return empty-handed from their sea expedition. Humiliated and enraged, they break camp, and, taking their sister with them, abandon Asdiwal.

He is picked up by strangers coming from Gitxatla, who are also on their way to the Nass for the candlefish season.

As in the previous case, they are a group of four brothers and a sister, whom Asdiwal wastes no time in marrying. They soon arrive together at the River Nass, where they sell large quantities of fresh meat and salmon to the Tsimshian, who have already settled there and are starving.

Since the catch that year is a good one, everyone goes home: the Tsimshian to their capital at Metlakatla and the Gitxatla to their town Laxalan, where Asdiwal, by this time rich and famous, has a son. One winter's day, he boasts that he can hunt sea-lions better than his brothers-in-law. They set out to sea together. Thanks to his magic objects, Asdiwal has a miraculously successful hunt on a reef, but is left there without food or fire by his angry brothers-in-law. A storm gets up and waves sweep over the rock. With the help of his father, who appears in time to save him, Asdiwal, transformed into a bird, succeeds in keeping himself above the waves, using his magic objects as a perch.

After two days and two nights the storm is calmed, and Asdiwal falls asleep exhausted. A mouse wakes him and leads him to the subterranean home of the sea-lions whom he has wounded, but who imagine (since Asdiwal's arrows are invisible to them) that they are victims of an epidemic. Asdiwal extracts the arrows and cures his hosts, whom he asks, in return, to guarantee his safe return. Unfortunately, the sea-lions' boats, which are made of their stomachs, are out of use, pierced by the hunter's arrows. The king of the sea-lions therefore lends Asdiwal his own stomach as a canoe and instructs him to send it back without delay. When he reaches

6

land, the hero discovers his wife, and his son alike, inconsolable. Thanks to the help of this good wife, but bad sister (for she carries out the rites which are essential to the success of the operation), Asdiwal makes killer-whales out of carved wood and brings them to life. They break open the boats with their fins and bring about the shipwreck and death of the wicked brothers-in-law.

But once again Asdiwal feels an irrepressible desire to revisit the scenes of his childhood. He leaves his wife and returns to the Skeena valley. He settles in the town of Ginadâos, where he is joined by his son, to whom he gives his magic bow and arrows, and from whom he receives a dog in return.

When winter comes, Asdiwal goes off to the mountains to hunt, but forgets his snow-shoes. Lost, and unable to go either up or down without them, he is turned to stone with his lance and his dog, and they can still be seen in that form at the peak of the great mountain by the lake of Ginadâos (Boas, 1912, pp. 71-146).

III

Let us keep provisionally to this version alone in order to attempt to define the essential points of its structure. The narrative refers to facts of various orders. First, the physical and political geography of the Tsimshian country, since the places and towns mentioned really do exist. Second, the economic life of the natives which, as we have seen, governs the great seasonal migrations between the Skeena and Nass Valleys, and during the course of which Asdiwal's adventures take place. Third, the social and family organization, for we witness several marriages, divorces, widowhoods, and other connected events. Lastly, the cosmology, for, unlike the others, two of Asdiwal's visits, one to heaven and the other below the earth, are of a mythological and not of an experiential order.

First of all, the geographical framework.

The story begins in the Skeena valley, when the two heroines leave their villages, one upstream, the other downstream, and meet half-way. In the version that Boas recorded at the Nass

7

Claude Lévi-Strauss

estuary (1902) it is stated that the meeting-place, this time on the Nass, is called Hwil-lê-ne-hwada, 'Where-they-met-each-other' (Boas, 1902, p. 225).

After her mother's death, the young woman and her son settle in her native village (i.e. her father's, where her mother had lived from the time of her marriage until her husband's death): the downstream village. It is from there that the visit to heaven takes place. This village, called Gitsalasert, 'People of the (Skeena) Canyon', is situated not far from the modern town of Usk (Garfield, 1939, p. 175; Boas, 1912, pp. 71, 276). Although the Tsimshian dialect was spoken there, it was outside the 'nine towns' which strictly speaking formed the Tsimshian province (Boas, 1912, p. 225).

On his mother's death, Asdiwal continues his journey down-stream, that is to say, westwards. He settles in the town of Ginaxangioget, where he marries. This is in proper Tsimshian country on the lower reaches of the Skeena. Ginaxangioget is in fact a term formed from the root of git = 'people' and $gi.k$ = 'hem-lock tree' from which comes $Ginax-angi.k$ 'the people of the firs' (Garfield, 1939, p. 175). And Ginaxangioget was one of the nine principal towns of the Tsimshian (Boas, 1916, pp. 482-483; Swanton, 1952, p. 606, gives 'Kinagingeet, near Metlakatla').

When Asdiwal leaves with his in-laws for the Nass to fish candlefish there, they go first by the Skeena estuary, then take to the sea, and stop at the capital city of the Tsimshian, Metlakatla – a recent town of the same name, founded by natives converted to Christianity, is to be found on Annette Island in Alaska (Beynon, 1941; Garfield, Wingert & Barbeau, 1951, pp. 33-34).

Old Metlakatla is on the coast, north of Prince Rupert and half-way between the Skeena and Nass estuaries. Ksemaksén, where the first quarrel takes place, and where Asdiwal is first abandoned by his brothers-in-law, is also on the coast, a little further north.

The Tsimshian-speaking tribe called Gitxatla, which is independent of those centres around Metlakatla, is a group of islanders living on Dolphin Island, south of the Skeena Estuary. Their name comes from git 'people' and $qxatla$ 'channel' (Garfield, 1939, p. 175. Also Boas, 1916, 483. Swanton, 1952,

8

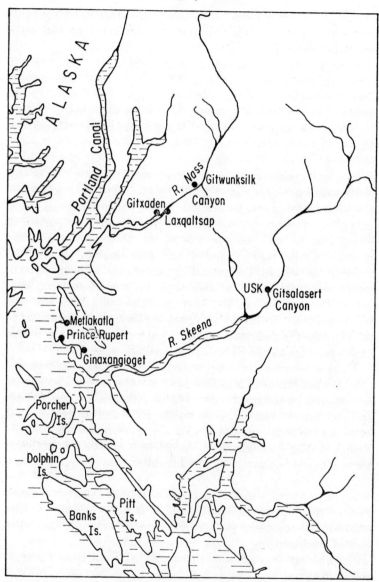

p. 607, gives 'Kitkatla, on Porcher Island'). Having travelled from East to West, Asdiwal accompanies them to the Nass, that is to say in a South-North direction, then in the opposite direction, to 'their town', off-shore from which (and probably to the West, since it was a deep-sea expedition) the visit to the sea-lions takes place.

From there, Asdiwal returns to the Skeena, that is to say this time from West to East. The story ends at Ginadâos, Ginadoiks perhaps, from *git* 'people', *na* 'of', *doiks* 'rapid current'; the name of a torrent which flows into the Skeena (Garfield, 1939, p. 176; cf. also Boas, 1912, p. 223: Ginadâiks, 'one of the nine towns of the Tsimshian').

Let us now consider the economic aspect. The activities of this order which are brought to notice by the myth are no less real than the geographical places and the populations evoked in the preceding paragraphs. Everything begins with a period of winter famine such as was well known to the natives in the period between mid-December and mid-January, before the moment at which, theoretically, the spring salmon arrived, which was just before the arrival of the candlefish; the period called 'the Interval' (Boas, 1916, pp. 398-399). After his visit to the heavens, Asdiwal takes part in the spring migrations to the Nass for the candlefish season; then we are told of the return of the families to the Skeena in the salmon season.

These seasonal variations – to use Marcel Mauss's expression – are on a par with other differences none the less real which are emphasized by the myth, notably that between the land-hunter (personified by Asdiwal, born on the river and upstream, that is to say inland) and the sea-hunter, personified first by the People of the Firs who live downstream on the estuary, and then, still more clearly, by the inhabitants of Dolphin Island.

When we move on to the sociological aspects, there is a much greater freedom of interpretation. It is not a question of an accurate documentary picture of the reality of native life, but a sort of counterpoint which seems sometimes to be in harmony with this reality, and sometimes to part from it in order to rejoin it again.

The initial sequence of events evokes clearly defined sociological conditions. The mother and daughter have been separated by the latter's marriage, and since that time each has lived with her own husband in his village. The elder woman's husband was also the father of the younger woman, who thus left her native village to follow her own husband upstream. We can recognize this as a society where, although there is a system of matrilineal filiation, residence is patrilocal, the wife going to live in her husband's village; and where the children, although they belong to their mother's clan, are brought up in their father's home and not in that of their maternal kin.

Such was the (real) situation among the Tsimshian. Boas emphasizes it several times: 'In olden times it was customary for a great chief to take a princess from each tribe to be his wife. Some had as many as sixteen or eighteen wives . . .' which would clearly be impossible if a man had to live in his wife's native village. More generally, says Boas: 'There is ample evidence showing that the young married people lived with the young man's parents', so that 'the children grew up in their father's home' (Boas, 1916, pp. 355, 529, 426; cf. also pp. 420, 427, 441, 499-500).

But, in the myth, this patrilocal type of residence is quickly undermined by famine, which frees the two women from their respective obligations and allows them, upon the death of their husbands, to meet (significantly enough) half-way. Their camping at the foot of the tree on the bank of the frozen river, equidistant from up-river and down-river, presents a picture of a matrilocal type of residence reduced to its simplest form, since the new household consists only of a mother and her daughter.

This reversal, which is barely hinted at, is all the more remarkable because all the subsequent marriages (in the myth) are going to be matrilocal, and thus contrary to the type found in reality.

First, Hatsenas's marriage with the younger woman. Fleeting though this union between a human being and a supernatural being may be, the husband still lives in his wife's home, and therefore in her mother's home. The matrilocal trend is even more apparent in the version recorded on the Nass. When his son Asi-hwil has grown up, Hatsenas (who here is called Hôux) says to his wife: 'Your brothers are coming to look for you. Therefore I must hide in the woods.' A short time after he had left, the brothers came, and left again the following morning,

11

laden with supplies of meat given to the women by their protector:

'As soon as they left, Hôux returned. The [women] told him that their brothers had asked them to return home. Then Hôux said "Let us part. You may return to your home; I will return to mine." On the following morning many people came to fetch the women and the boy. They took them to Gitxaden. The boy's uncles gave a feast and his mother told them the boy's name, Asi-hwil . . .' (Boas, 1902, p. 227).

Not only does the husband seem an intruder, regarded with suspicion by his brothers-in-law, and afraid that they might attack him, but, contrary to what (really) happens among the Tsimshian and in other societies characterized by the association of matrilineal filiation and patrilocal residence (Boas, 1916, p. 423; Malinowski, 1932), the food gifts go from the sister's husband to the wife's brothers.

Matrilocal marriage, accompanied by antagonism between the husband and his in-laws, is further illustrated by Asdiwal's marriage to Evening-Star; they live in her father's home, and the father-in-law shows so much hostility towards his son-in-law that he sets him trials which are deemed to be fatal.

Matrilocal, too, is Asdiwal's second marriage in the land of the People of the Firs, which is accompanied by hostility between the husband and his brothers-in-law because they abandon him and persuade their sister to follow them.

The same theme is expressed in the third marriage in the land of the People of the Channel, at any rate to start with. For after Asdiwal's visit to the sea-lions the situation is reversed: Asdiwal recovers his wife, who had refused to follow her brothers, and was wandering in search of her husband. What is more, she collaborates with him to produce the 'machination' – in the literal and the figurative sense – by means of which he takes revenge on his brothers-in-law. Finally, patrilocality triumphs when Asdiwal abandons his wife (whereas, in the previous marriages, it had been his wife who had abandoned him) and returns to the Skeena where he was born, and where his son comes alone to join him. Thus having begun with the story of the *reunion of a mother and her daughter*, freed from their affines or *paternal kin*, the myth ends with the story of the *reunion of a father and his son*, freed from their affines or *maternal kin*.

But if the initial and final sequences in the myth constitute from a sociological point of view a pair of oppositions, the same is true, from a cosmological point of view, of the two supernatural voyages which interrupt the hero's 'real' journey. The first voyage takes him to the heavens, and into the home of the Sun, who first tries to kill him and then agrees to bring him back to life. The second takes Asdiwal to the subterranean kingdom of the sea-lions, whom he has himself killed or wounded, but whom he agrees to look after and to cure. The first voyage results in a marriage which, as we have seen, is matrilocal, and which, moreover, bears witness to a maximal exogamous separation (between an earth-born man and a woman from heaven). But this marriage will be broken up by Asdiwal's infidelity with a woman of his own village, which may be seen as a suggestion of a marriage which, if it really took place, would, so to speak, neutralize matri-locality (since husband and wife would come from the same place) and would be characterized by an endogamous proximity which would also be maximal (marriage within the village). It is true that the hero's second supernatural voyage, to the subterranean kingdom of the sea-lions, does not lead to a marriage, but in any case, as has already been shown, this visit brings about a reversal in the matrilocal tendency of Asdiwal's successive marriages, for it separates his third wife from her brothers, the hero himself from his wife, their son from his mother, and leaves only one relationship in existence: that between the father and his son.

IV

In this analysis of the myth, we have distinguished four levels: the geographic, the techno-economic, the sociological, and the cosmological. The first two are exact transcriptions of reality; the fourth has nothing to do with it, and in the third, real and imaginary institutions are interwoven. Yet in spite of these differences, the levels cannot be separated out by the native

mind. It is rather that everything happens as if the levels were
provided with different codes, each being used according to the
needs of the moment, and according to its particular capacity,
to transmit the same message. It is the nature of this message
that we shall now consider.

Winter famines are a recurrent event in the economic life of
the Tsimshian. But the famine which starts the story off is
also a cosmological theme. All along the Northwest Pacific
Coast, in fact, the present state of the universe is attributed to
the havoc wrought in the original order by the demiurge Giant
or Raven (Txamsen, in Tsimshian) during travels which he
undertook in order to satisfy his irrepressible voracity. Thus
Txamsem is perpetually in a state of famine, and famine,
although a negative condition, is seen as the *'primum movens'*
of Creation.[4] In this sense we can say that the hunger of the
two women in our myth has a cosmic significance; these
heroines are not so much legendary persons as incarnations of
principles which are at the origin of place-names.

One may schematize the initial situation as follows:

| Mother | (is opposed to) Daughter |
| Elder | („ „ „) Younger |
| Downstream („ „ „) Upstream |
| West | („ „ „) East |
| South | („ „ „) North |

The meeting takes place at the half-way point, a situation
which, as we have seen, corresponds to a neutralization of
patrilocal residence and to the fulfilment of the conditions for a
matrilocal residence which is as yet only hinted at. But since
the mother dies on the very spot where the meeting and the
birth of Asdiwal took place, the essential movement, which her
daughter begins by leaving the village of her marriage 'very
far upstream' (Boas, 1912, p. 71), is in the direction East-West,
as far as her native village in the Skeena Canyon, where she in
her turn dies, leaving the field open for the hero.

Asdiwal's first adventure presents us with an opposition:
heaven/earth which the hero is able to surmount by virtue of
the intervention of his father, Hatsenas, the bird of good omen.
The latter is a creature of the atmospheric or middle heaven and
consequently well qualified to play the role of mediator between

the earth-born Asdiwal and his father-in-law the Sun, ruler of the highest heaven. Even so, Asdiwal does not manage to overcome his earthly nature, to which he twice submits, first in yielding to the charms of a fellow-countrywoman and then in yielding to nostalgia for his home village. Thus there remains a series of unresolved oppositions:

Low	High
Earth	Heaven
Man	Woman
Endogamy	Exogamy

Pursuing his course westwards, Asdiwal contracts a second matrilocal marriage which generates a new series of oppositions:

Mountain-hunting	Sea-hunting
Land	Water

These oppositions too are insurmountable, and Asdiwal's earthly nature carries him away a third time, with the result that he is abandoned by his wife and his brothers-in-law.

Asdiwal contracts his last marriage not with the river-dwellers, but with islanders, and the same conflict is repeated. The opposition continues to be insurmountable, although at each stage the terms more closer together. This time it is in fact a question of a quarrel between Asdiwal and his brothers-in-law on the occasion of a hunt on a reef when the seas are running high; that is to say, on land and water at the same time. In the previous incident, Asdiwal and his brothers-in-law had gone their separate ways, one inland and on foot, the others out to sea and in boats. This time they go together in boats, and it is only when they land that Asdiwal's superiority is made manifest by the use he makes of the magic objects intended for mountain-hunting:

'It was a very difficult hunt on account of the waves which swept past [the reef] in the direction of the open sea. While they were speaking about this, [Asdiwal] said: "My dear fellows I have only to put on my snowshoes and I'll run up the rocks you are talking about".' He succeeds in this way, whilst his brothers-in-law, incapable of landing, stay shame-facedly in their boats (Boas, 1912, pp. 125-126).

Asdiwal, the earth-born master of the hunt, finds himself abandoned on a reef in high seas; he has come to the furthest point of his westward journey; so much for the geographic and economic aspects. But, from a logical point of view, his adventures can be seen in a different form – that of a series of impossible mediations between oppositions which are ordered in a descending scale: high and low, water and earth, sea-hunting and mountain-hunting, etc.

Consequently, on the spatial plane, the hero is completely led off his course, and his failure is expressed in this *maximal separation* from his starting-point. On the logical plane, he has also failed because of his immoderate attitude towards his brothers-in-law, and by his inability to play the role of a mediator, even though the last of the oppositions which had to be overcome – between the types of life led by the land- and sea-hunters – is reduced to a *minimal separation*. There would seem to be a dead end at this point; but from neutral the myth goes into reverse and its machinery starts up again.

The king of the mountains (in Nass dialect, Asdiwal is called Asi-hwil, which means 'Crosser of Mountains') is caught on a mockery of a mountain, and doubly so because, on the one hand, it is nothing more than a reef and, on the other, it is surrounded and almost submerged by the sea. The ruler of wild animals and killer of bears is to be saved by a she-mouse, a mockery of a wild animal.[5] She makes him undertake a *subterranean journey*, just as the she-bear, the supreme wild animal, had imposed on Asdiwal a *celestial journey*. In fact, the only thing that is missing is for the mouse to change into a woman and to offer the hero a marriage which would be symmetrical to the other, but opposite to it; and although this element is not to be found in any of the versions, we know at least that the mouse is a fairy: Lady Mouse-woman, as she is called in the texts, where the word *ksem*, a term of respect addressed to a woman, is prefixed to the word denoting a rodent. Following through the inversion more systematically than had been possible under the preceding hypothesis, this fairy is an old woman incapable of procreation: an 'inverse wife'.

And that is not all. The man who had killed animals in their hundreds goes this time to heal them and win their love.[6] The

16

bringer of food (who repeatedly exercises the power he received from his father in this respect for the benefit of his family) becomes food, since he is transported in the sea-lion's stomach.[7]

Finally, the visit to the subterranean world (which is also, in many respects, an 'upside-down world') sets the course of the hero's return, for from then onwards he travels from West to East, from the sea towards the mainland, from the salt water of the ocean to the fresh water of the Skeena.

This overall reversal does not affect the development of the plot, which unfolds up to the final catastrophe. When Asdiwal returns to his people and to the initial patrilocal situation, he takes up his favourite occupation again, helped by his magic objects. But he *forgets* one of them, and this mistake is fatal. After a successful hunt, he finds himself trapped half-way up the mountain-side: 'Where might he go now? He could not go up, he could not go down, he could not go to either side' (Boas, 1912, p. 145). And on the spot he is changed to stone, that is to say paralysed, reduced to his earth-born nature in the stony and unchangeable form in which he has been seen 'for generations'.

v

The above analysis leads us to draw a distinction between two aspects of the construction of a myth: the sequences and the schemata (*schèmes*).[8] The sequences form the apparent content of the myth; the chronological order in which things happen: the meeting of the two women, the intervention of the supernatural protector, the birth of Asdiwal, his childhood, his visit to heaven, his successive marriages, his hunting and fishing expeditions, his quarrels with his brothers-in-law, etc.

But these sequences are organized, on planes at different levels (of abstraction), in accordance with schemata, which exist simultaneously, superimposed one upon another; just as a melody composed for several voices is held within bounds by constraints in two dimensions, first by its own melodic line which is horizontal, and second by the contrapuntal schemata (settings) which are vertical. Let us then draw up an inventory of such schemata for this present myth.

1. *Geographic Schema.* The hero goes from East to West, then

he returns from West to East. This return journey is modulated by another one, from the South to the North and then from the North to the South, which corresponds to the seasonal migrations of the Tsimshian (in which the hero takes part) to the River Nass for the candlefish season in the spring, then to the Skeena for the salmon-fishing in the summer.

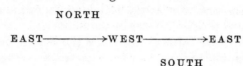

NORTH

EAST————————→WEST————————→EAST

SOUTH

2. *Cosmological Schema.* Three supernatural visits establish a relationship between terms thought of respectively as 'below' and 'above': the visit to the young widow by Hatsenas, the bird of good omen associated with the atmospheric heavens; the visit by Asdiwal to the highest heavens in pursuit of Evening-Star; his visit to the subterranean kingdom of the sea-lions under the guidance of Lady Mouse-woman. The end of Asdiwal, trapped in the mountain, then appears as a *neutralization* of the intermediate mediation (between atmospheric heaven and earth) established at his birth but which even so does not enable him to bring off two further extreme mediations (the one between heaven and earth considered as the opposition low/high and the other between the sea and the land considered as the opposition East/West):

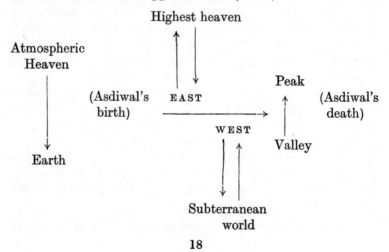

3. *Integration.* The above two schemata are integrated in a third consisting of several binary oppositions, none of which the hero can resolve, although the distance separating the opposed terms gradually dwindles. The initial and final oppositions: high/low and peak/valley are 'vertical' and thus belong to the cosmological schema. The two intermediate oppositions (water/land and sea-hunting/mountain-hunting) are 'horizontal' and belong to the geographic schema. But in fact the final opposition (peak/valley), which is also the narrowest contrast, brings into association the essential characteristics of the two preceding schemata: it is 'vertical' in form but 'geographical' in content. This double aspect, natural and supernatural, of the opposition between peak and valley is already specified in the myth, since the hero's perilous situation is the result of an earthquake brought about by the gods (see below, p. 22). Asdiwal's failure (in that, because he forgot his snow-shoes, he is trapped half-way up the mountain) thus takes on a threefold significance: geographical, cosmological, and logical:

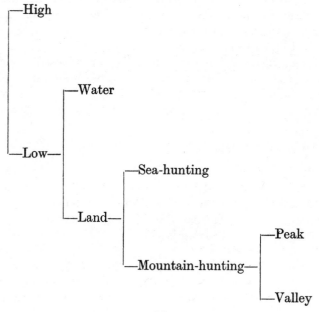

When the three schemata are reduced to their bare essentials in this way, retaining only the order and amplitude of the oppositions, their complementarity becomes apparent.

Schema 1 is composed of a sequence of oscillations of constant amplitude: East – North – West – South – East.

Schema 2 starts at a zero point (the meeting half-way between upstream and downstream) and is followed by an oscillation of medium amplitude (atmospheric heavens – earth), then by oscillations of maximum amplitude (earth – heaven, heaven – earth, earth – subterranean world, subterranean world – earth) which die away at the zero point (half-way up, between peak and valley).

Schema 3 begins with an oscillation of maximum amplitude (high-low) which dies away in a series of oscillations of decreasing amplitude (water – land; sea-hunting – mountain-hunting; valley – peak).

4. *Sociological Schema.* To start with, patrilocal residence prevails. It gives way progressively to matrilocal residence (Hatsenas's marriage), which becomes murderous (Asdiwal's marriage in heaven), then merely hostile (the marriage in the land of the People of the Firs), before weakening and finally reversing (marriage among the People of the Channel) to allow a return to patrilocal residence.

The sociological schema has not, however, a closed structure like the geographic schema, since, at the beginning, it involves a mother and her daughter, in the middle, a husband, his wife, and his brothers-in-law, and, at the end, a father and his son.[9]

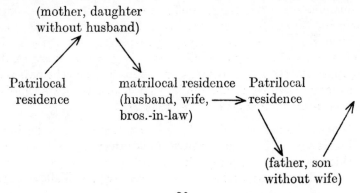

5. *Techno-economic Schema.* The myth begins by evoking a winter famine; it ends with a successful hunt. In between, the story follows the (real-life) economic cycle and the seasonal migrations of the native fishermen:

	Fishing	Salmon	Successful
Famine—→	for —→	Fishing—→	Hunt
	Candlefish		

6. *Global Integration.* If the myth is finally reduced to its two extreme propositions, the initial state of affairs and the final, which together summarize its operational function, then we end up with a simplified diagram:

(Initial State)		(Final State)	
FEMALE		MALE	
EAST-WEST	axis	HIGH-LOW	axis
FAMINE		REPLETION	
MOVEMENT		IMMOBILITY	

Having separated out the codes, we have analysed the structure of the message. It now remains to decipher the meaning.

VI

In Boas (1916) there is a version of the story of Asdiwal that is remarkable in several respects. First, it brings a new character into play: Waux, the son of Asdiwal's second marriage, who seems to be a doublet of his father, although his adventures take place after those of Asdiwal. In chronological order, they form supplementary sequences of events. But these *later* sequences are organized in schemata which are at the same time *homologous* to those which have been described and more *explicit* than them. Everything seems to suggest that, as it draws to its close, the obvious narrative (the sequences) tends to approach the latent content of the myth (the schemata); a convergence which is not unlike that which the listener discovers in the final chords of a symphony.

> When Asdiwal's second wife (his first earth-born wife) bore him a son, he was called Waux. That means 'very light', for this son used to fly away like a spark.[10]
> The father and son loved each other very much and always

21

hunted together. And thus it was a cause of great sorrow to Waux when his uncles forced him to follow them after they had left his father (Asdiwal) at Ksemaksén. The mother and son had even secretly tried to find Asdiwal and had only abandoned the attempt when they were convinced that he must have been devoured by some wild animal.

Waux, following in his father's footsteps, became a great hunter. Before his mother died, she made him marry a cousin, and the young couple lived happily. Waux continued to hunt on his father's hunting-grounds, sometimes in company with his wife, who gave birth to twins.

Soon Waux's children went hunting with him, as he had formerly done with his father. One day he went with them into an unexplored region. The children slipped on the mountain and were both killed. The following year Waux returned to the same place to hunt, armed with all the magic objects he had inherited from his father, except the lance, which he forgot. Taken unawares by an earthquake, he tried in vain to make his wife (whom he saw in the valley) understand that he needed her ritual help. He shouted to her to sacrifice fat to the supernatural powers in order to appease them. But the wife could not hear and misunderstood, repeating not what her husband had said, but what she wanted to do herself, 'You want me to eat fat?' Discouraged, Waux agreed, and his wife sated herself with fat and cold water. Satisfied, she lay down on an old log. Her body broke apart and was changed into a veined flint which is still found all over that place today.

Waux, because he had forgotten the lance which enabled him to split the rock and open a way through the mountain, and having lost his last chance of placating the elements because of the misunderstanding which had arisen between his wife and himself, was turned to stone, as were also his dog and all his magic objects. They are still there to this day (Boas, 1916, pp. 243-245).

Several significant permutations will be noticed if this is compared with the version which we have taken as a point of reference.

Asdiwal had an only son (in fact, as we have seen, two only sons, born of consecutive marriages and confused into one single one in the story), whereas Waux has twins. We do not know much about these twins, but it is tempting to set up a parallel between them and the two magic dogs that Asi-hwil was given by his father in the River Nass version: one red, the other spotted – that is, marked by a contrast which suggests (when compared with the symbolic colour systems so common among the North American Indians) divergent functions.

Moreover, the existence of twins already provides a pointer. In the American series of mediators, twins represent the weakest term, and come at the bottom of the list, after the Messiah (who unites opponents) and the trickster (in whom they are in juxtaposition). The pair of twins brings opposites into association but at the same time leaves them individually distinct (see Lévi-Strauss, 1963a, Ch. XI, 'The Structural Study of Myth').

The change from a single mediator to a pair of twins is thus a sign of a weakening in the function of the mediator, all the clearer because only shortly after their appearance on the mystical scene the twins die in unexplored territory without having played any part.

Like Asdiwal, Waux ends by being turned to stone as a result of forgetting a magic object; the identity of this object, however, changes from one version to another. In Asdiwal, it is the snow-shoes; in Waux the lance. These magic objects are the instruments of mediation given to the hero by his supernatural father. Here, again, there is a gradation; the snow-shoes make it possible to climb up and down the steepest slopes; the lance enables its owner to go straight through walls of rock. The lance is thus a more radical means than the snow-shoes, which come to terms with the obstacle rather than doing away with it. Waux's omission seems more serious than Asdiwal's. The weaker mediator loses the stronger instrument of mediation and his powers are doubly diminished as a result.

Thus the story of Waux follows a dialectic regression; but, in another sense, it reveals a progression, since it is with this variant that a structure which had remained open in certain respects is finally closed.

Waux's wife dies of *repletion*. That is the end of a story which opened by showing Asdiwal's (or Asi-hwil's) mother a victim of *starvation*. It was this famine which set her in *motion*, just as, now, abuse of food brings Waux's wife to a *halt*. And before leaving this point let us note that in fact the two characters of the initial sequence were two women who were *single, unfed*, and *on the move*, whereas those of the final sequence were a *couple* composed of a husband and his wife, one a *bringer of food* (who is not understood) and the other *overfed* (because she does not understand), and both *paralysed* in spite of this opposition (but also perhaps because of the negative complementarity that it expresses).

The most important transformation is that represented by the marriage of Waux. It has been seen that Asdiwal contracted a series of marriages, all equally unsuccessful. He cannot choose between his supernatural bride and his fellow-country-women; he is abandoned (though against her will, it is true) by his Tsimshian spouse. His Gitxatla wife remains faithful to him and even goes so far as to betray her brothers; it is he who abandons her. He ends his days, having joined forces with his son again, in a celibate state.

Waux, on the other hand, marries only once, but this marriage proves fatal for him. Here, however, it is a case of a marriage *arranged* by Waux's mother (unlike Asdiwal's *adventurous* marriages) and a marriage with a *cousin* (whereas Asdiwal marries complete *strangers*), or more precisely, with his cross-cousin, his mother's brother's daughter (which explains the intermediary role played by his mother).[11]

As Boas explains in the text quoted in the footnote above, there was a preference for marriage with the mother's brother's daughter among the Tsimshian, especially in the noble classes from which our heroes are drawn. Garfield doubts whether the practice was strictly in accordance with mythical models (Garfield, 1939, pp. 232-233), but the point is of secondary importance, since we are studying schemata with a normative function. In a society like that of the Tsimshian, there is no difficulty in seeing why this type of marriage could be thought ideal. Boys grew up in their fathers' homes, but sooner or later they had to go over to their maternal uncle when they inherited his titles, prerogatives, and hunting-grounds (Boas, 1916, p. 411, where he contradicts p. 401. We shall return to this contradiction later.) Marriage with the matrilateral cousin provided a solution to this conflict.

Furthermore, as has often been found to be the case in other societies of the same type, such a marriage made it possible to overcome another conflict: that between the patrilineal and matrilineal tendencies of Tsimshian society, which, as we have seen above, is very deeply conscious of the two lines (p. 3. See also on this point E. Sapir, 1915, pp. 6 and 27, and Garfield, Wingert & Barbeau, 1951, pp. 17-25). By means of such a marriage, a man ensures the continued existence of his hereditary privileges and of such titles as he might have within the limits of a small family circle (Swanton, 1909; Wedgewood, 1928; Richards, 1914).

I have shown elsewhere that it is unlikely that this interpretation may be seen as the universal origin of cross-cousin marriage (Lévi-Strauss, 1949, pp. 158-159). But in the case of a society which has feudal tendencies, it certainly corresponds to real motives which contributed to the survival, or to the adoption, of the custom. The final explanation of this custom must, however, be sought in those characteristics which are common to all societies which practised it.

The Tsimshian myths provide, furthermore, a surprising commentary on the native theory of marriage with the matrilateral cross-cousin in the story of the princess who refuses to marry her cousin (her father's sister's son).

No less cruel than she was proud, the princess demands that her cousin prove his love by disfiguring himself. He slashes his face and then she rejects him because of his ugliness. Reduced to a state of despair, the young man seeks death and ventures into the land of Chief Pestilence, master of deformities. After the hero has undergone rigorous trials, the chief agrees to transform him into a Prince Charming.

Now his cousin is passionately attracted to him, and the young man, in his turn, demands that she sacrifice her beauty, but only in order to heap sarcasm upon her head. The now hideous princess tries to move Chief Pestilence to pity, and at once the maimed and deformed race of people who make

up his court set upon the unfortunate woman, break her
bones and tear her apart.

Boas's informant sees in this tale the myth which lies at the
origin of the rites and ceremonies celebrated at the marriages
of cross-cousins.

'There was a custom among our people that the nephew of
the chief had to marry the chief's daughter, because the tribe
of the chief wanted the chief's nephew to be the heir of his
uncle and to inherit his place after his death. This custom
has gone on, generation after generation, all along until now,
and the places of the head men have thus been inherited.'

But, the informant goes on, it is because of the disaster that
struck the rebellious princess that it was decided that on such
occasions 'no young woman should have any say about her
marriage. . . . Even though the young woman does not want to
marry the man, she has to consent when the agreement has
been made on both sides to marry them' (that is to say after
negotiations between the maternal descent groups of the young
people).

'When the prince and princess have married, the tribe of
the young man's uncle mobilize. Then the tribe of the young
woman's uncle also mobilize and they have a fight. The two
parties cast stones at each other, and the heads of many of
those on each side are hit. The scars made by the stones on
the heads of each chief's people are signs of the marriage
pledge'.[12]

In his commentary Boas notes that this myth is not peculiar
to the Tsimshian, but is found also among the Tlingit and the
Haida, who are likewise matrilineal and likewise faithful to the
same type of marriage. Thus it is clear that it portrays a
fundamental aspect of the social organization of these peoples,
which consists in a hostile equilibrium between the matrilineal
lineages of the village chiefs. In a system of generalized
exchange, such as results, in these feudal families, from the
preferential marriage with the mother's brother's daughter, the

families are, so to speak, ranged around a more or less stable circle, in such a way that each family occupies, at least temporarily, the position of 'wife-giver' with respect to some other family and of 'wife-taker' with respect to a third. Depending on the society, this lopsided structure (lopsided, because there is no guarantee that in giving one will receive) can achieve a certain equilibrium – more apparent, however, than real – in several ways: democratically, by following the principle that all marriage exchanges are equivalent; or, on the contrary, by stipulating that one of the positions (wife-giver, wife-taker) is, by definition, superior to the other. But given a different social and economic context, this amounts in theory, if not in practice, to the same thing, since each family must occupy both positions (Lévi-Strauss, 1949; 1963a, pp. 311-312). The societies of the Northwest Pacific Coast could not, or would not, choose one of these points of balance, and the respective superiority or inferiority of the groups involved was openly contested on the occasion of each marriage. Each marriage, along with the potlatches which accompanied and preceded it, and the transfers of titles and property occasioned by it, provided the means by which the groups concerned might gain an advantage over each other while at the same time putting an end to former disputes. It was necessary to make peace but only on the best possible terms. French mediaeval society offers, in terms of patrilineal institutions, a symmetrical picture of a situation which had much in common with the one just described.

In such circumstances, is there anything amazing about the horrid little story in which the natives see the origin of their marriage institutions? Is there anything surprising in the fact that the ceremony of marriage between first cousins takes the form of a bloody battle? When we believe that, in bringing to light these antagonisms which are inherent in the structure of Tsimshian society, we are 'reaching rock bottom' (in the words of Marcel Mauss), we express in this geological metaphor an approach that has many points of comparison with that made by the myths of Asdiwal and Waux. All the paradoxes conceived by the native mind, on the most diverse planes: geographic, economic, sociological, and even cosmological, are, when all is said and done, assimilated to that less obvious yet so real paradox which marriage with the matrilateral cousin attempts but fails to resolve. But the failure is *admitted* in our myths, and there precisely lies their function.

Let us glance at them again in this light. The winter famine which kills the husbands of the two original heroines frees them from patrilocal residence and enables them first to meet and then to return to the daughter's native village, which will correspond, for her son, to a matrilocal type of residence. Thus a shortage of food is related to the sending out of young women, who return to their own descent groups when food is scarce. This is symbolic of an event which is illustrated in a more concrete fashion each year, even if there is no famine, by the departure of the candlefish from the Nass and then of the salmon from the Skeena. These fish come from the open sea, arrive from the South and the West, and go up the rivers in an easterly direction. Like the departing fish, Asdiwal's mother continues her journey westwards and towards the sea, where Asdiwal discovers the disastrous effects of matrilocal marriage.

The first of his marriages is with Evening-Star, who is a supernatural being. The correlation of female heaven and male earth which is implicit in this event is interesting from two points of view.

First, Asdiwal is in a way fished up by the She-Bear who draws him up to heaven, and the myths often describe grizzly bears as *fishing for salmon*.[13] Like a salmon too, Asdiwal is fished up in a net by the compassionate Sun after he has crashed to earth.[14] But when Asdiwal returns from his symmetrically opposite visit to the subterranean kingdom of the sea-lions, he travels in one of their stomachs, like a food; comparable to the *candlefish* which are scooped up from the bed of the River Nass, the 'Stomach River'. Furthermore, the hero now goes in the opposite direction, no longer from East to West like the food disappearing, but from West to East like the food returning.

Second, this reversal is accompanied by another: from matrilocal to patrilocal residence; and this reversal is in itself a variable of the replacement of a celestial journey by a subterranean one, which brings Asdiwal from the position of: earth, male, dominated, to that of: earth, male, dominant.

Patrilocal residence is no more successful for Asdiwal. He gets his son back but loses his wife and his affines. Isolated in this new relationship, and incapable of bringing together the two types of filiation and residence, he is stuck half-way at the moment when he has almost reached his goal; at the end of a successful hunt, he has reconquered food but lost his freedom of movement. Famine, which causes movement, has given way to abundance, but at the price of paralysis.

We can then now better understand how Waux's marriage with his matrilateral cousin, following that of his father, symbolizes the futile last attempts of Tsimshian thought and Tsimshian society to overcome their inherent contradictions. For this marriage fails as the result of a *misunderstanding* added to an *omission*: Waux had succeeded in staying with his maternal kin while at the same time retaining his father's hunting-grounds; he had managed to inherit in both the maternal and the paternal lines at the same time; but, although they are cousins, he and his wife remain alienated from one another, because cross-cousin marriage, in a feudal society, is a palliative and a decoy. In these societies, women are always objects of exchange, but property is also a cause of battle.

VII

The above analysis suggests an observation of a different kind: it is always rash to undertake, as Boas wanted to do in his monumental *Tsimshian Mythology*, 'a description of the life, social organization and religious ideas and practices of a people . . . as it appears from their mythology' (Boas, 1916, p. 32).

The myth is certainly related to given (empirical) facts, but not as a *re-presentation* of them. The relationship is of a dialectic kind, and the institutions described in the myths can be the very opposite of the real institutions. This will in fact always be the case when the myth is trying to express a negative truth. As has already been seen, the story of Asdiwal has landed the great American ethnologist in no little difficulty, for Waux is there said to have inherited his father's hunting-grounds, while other texts, as well as eye-witness observation, reveal that a man's property, including his hunting-grounds, went to his sister's son, that is to say from man to man in the maternal line.[15]

But Waux's paternal inheritance no more reflects real conditions than do his father's matrilocal marriages. In real life, the children grew up in the patrilocal home. Then they went to finish their education at their maternal uncle's home; after marrying, they returned to live with their parents, bringing their wives with them, and they settled in their uncle's village only when they were called upon to succeed him. Such, at any rate, was the case among the nobility, whose mythology formed a real 'court literature'. The comings and goings were one of the outward signs of the tensions between lineages connected by marriage. Mythical speculation about types of residence which are exclusively patrilocal or matrilocal do not therefore have anything to do with the reality of the structure of Tsimshian society, but rather with its inherent possibilities and its latent potentialities. Such speculations, in the last analysis, do not seek to depict what is real, but to justify the shortcomings of reality, since the extreme positions are only *imagined* in order to show that they are *untenable*. This step, which is fitting for mythical thought, implies an admission (but in the veiled language of the myth) that the social facts when thus examined are marred by an insurmountable contradiction. A contradiction which, like the hero of the myth, Tsimshian society cannot understand and prefers to forget.

This conception of the relation of the myth to reality no doubt limits the use of the former as a documentary source. But it opens the way for other possibilities; for in abandoning the search for a constantly accurate picture of ethnographic reality in the myth, we gain, on occasions, a means of reaching unconscious categories.

A moment ago it was recalled that Asdiwal's two journeys – from East to West and from West to East – were correlated with types of residence, respectively matrilocal and patrilocal. But in fact the Tsimshian have patrilocal residence, and from this we can (and indeed must) draw the conclusion that one of the orientations corresponds to the direction implicit in a real-life 'reading' of their institutions, the other to the opposite direction. The journey from West to East, the return journey, is accompanied by a return to patrilocality. Therefore the direction in which it is made is, for the native mind, the only real direction, the other being purely imaginary.

That is, moreover, what the myth proclaims. The move to the East assures Asdiwal's return to his element, the Earth, and to his native land. When he went westwards it was as a bringer of food putting an end to starvation; he made up for the absence of food while at the same time travelling in the same direction as that taken by food when it departed. Journeying in the opposite direction, in the sea-lion's stomach, he is symbolically identified with food, and he travels in the direction in which the food (of actual experience) returns.

The same applies to matrilocal residence; it is introduced as a negative reality, to make up for the non-existence of patrilocal residence caused by the death of the husbands.

What then is the West–East direction in native thought? It is the direction taken by the candlefish and the salmon when they arrive from the sea each year to enter the rivers and race upstream. If this orientation is also that which the Tsimshian must adopt in order to obtain an undistorted picture of their concrete social existence, is it not because they see themselves as being *sub specie piscis*; that they put themselves in the fishes' place, or rather that they put the fish in their place?

This hypothesis, arrived at by a process of deductive reasoning, is indirectly confirmed by ritual institutions and mythology.

Fishing and the preparation of the fish are the occasion for all kinds of ritual among the natives of the Northwest Coast. We have already seen that the women must use their naked breasts to press the candlefish in order to extract the oil from it, and that the remains must be left to rot near the dwellings in spite of the smell. The salmon does not rot, since it is dried in the sun or smoked. But there are further ritual conditions which must be observed: for instance, it must be cut up with a primitive knife made of a mussel shell, and any kind of stone, bone, or metal blade is forbidden. Women set about this operation sitting on the ground with their legs apart (Boas, 1916, pp. 449-450 and 919-932 (Nootka)).

These prohibitions and prescriptions seem to represent the same intention: to bring out the immediacy of the relationship between fish and man by treating fish as if it were a man, or at any rate by ruling out, or limiting to the extreme, the use of manufactured objects which are part of culture; or, in other words, by denying or underestimating the differences between fish and men.

The myths, for their part, tell of the visit of a prince to the kingdom of the salmon, whence he returns, having won their alliance, himself transformed into a fish. All these myths have one incident in common: the prince is welcomed by the salmon and learns that he may in no circumstances eat the same food as they, but must not hesitate to kill and eat the fish themselves, regardless of the fact that they thenceforth appear to him in human form (Boas, 1916, pp. 192-206, 770-778, 919-932).

It is at this point that the mythical identification hits upon the only real relationship between fish and men: one of food. It persists, even in the myth, as an alternative: either to eat like salmon (although one is a man) or to eat salmon (although they are like men). This latter solution is the right one, and thanks to it they are reborn from their bones, which had been carefully collected and then immersed or burned. But the first solution would be an *abuse of identification*, of man with salmon, not of salmon with man. The character in the myth who was guilty of this was transformed into a root or a rock – like Asdiwal – condemned to immobility and perpetually bound to the earth.

Starting with an initial situation characterized by irrepressible movement, and ending in a final situation characterized by perpetual immobility, the myth of Asdiwal expresses in its own way a fundamental aspect of the native philosophy. The start presents us with the absence of food; and everything which has been said above leads us to think that the role of Asdiwal, as bringer of food, consists in (bringing about) a negation of this absence, but that is quite another thing from (saying that Asdiwal's role equates with) the presence of food. In fact, when this presence is finally obtained, with Asdiwal taking on the aspect of 'food itself' (and no longer that of 'bringer of food'), the result is a state of inertia.

But starvation is no more a tolerable human condition than is

immobility. Therefore we must conclude that for these natives
the only positive form of existence is a *negation of non-existence*.
It is out of the question to develop this theory within the limits
of the present work. But let us note in passing that it would
shed new light on the *need for self-assertion* which, in the
potlatch, the feasts, the ceremonies, and the feudal rivalries,
seems to be such a particular characteristic of the societies of
the Northwest Pacific Coast.

VIII

There is one last problem which remains to be solved, that which
is posed by the differences between the Nass River version and
those recorded on the coast, in which the action takes place
on the Skeena. Up to now we have followed these latter ones,
which are very similar to each other. Boas even says that the
two versions are 'practically identical'.[16] Let us now look at the
Nass version.

> Famine reigns in the two villages of Laxqaltsap and
> Gitwunksilk – it is possible to place them: the first is the
> present Greenville on the Nass estuary,[17] and the second is
> on the lower Nass, but further upstream.[18] Two sisters,
> separated by marriage, each live in one of the villages. They
> decide to join forces, and meet half-way in a place which is
> named in memory of this event. They have a few provisions.
> The sister from down-river has only a few hawberries, the one
> from up-river, a small piece of spawn. They share this and
> bewail their plight.
> One of the sisters – the one from up-river – has come with
> her daughter, who does not enter the story again. The one
> from down-river, the younger of the two, is still unmarried.
> A stranger visits her at night. He is called Hôux, which means
> 'Good Luck'. When he learns of the state of the women, he
> miraculously provides food for them, and the younger
> woman soon gives birth to a son, Asi-hwil, for whom his
> father makes a pair of snow-shoes. At first they are useless,
> but once perfected, they bestow magic powers on their
> wearer. Asi-hwil's father also gives him two magic dogs, and

33

a lance which can pass through rock. From then on, the hero reveals himself to be a better hunter than other supernatural beings against whom he is matched.

Then follows the episode of Hôux's retreat from his brothers-in-law which has been summarized above (see pp. 11-12). They carry off their sister and their nephew at Gitxaden, down-stream from Nass Canyon.[19] There, the hero is drawn towards the sky by the slave of a supernatural being, disguised as a white bear; but he does not succeed in reaching the heavenly abode and returns to earth having lost track of the bear.

He then goes to Tsimshian country, where he marries the sister of the sea-lion hunters. He humiliates them by his superiority, is abandoned by them, visits the sea-lions in their subterranean kingdom, looks after them and cures them, gets a canoe made of their intestines which brings him back to the coast, where he kills his brothers-in-law with artificial killer-whales. He finds his wife and never leaves her again (Boas, 1902, pp. 225-229).

Clearly, this version is very poor. It has very few episodes, and when compared with Boas (1912) which has been our point of reference up to now, the sequence of events seems very confused. It would, however, be quite wrong to treat the Nass version simply as a weakened echo of the Skeena ones. In the best-preserved part, the initial sequence of events, it is as if the richness of detail had been preserved, but at the cost of permutations which, without any doubt, form a system. Let us therefore begin by listing them, distinguishing the elements which are common to both versions from the elements which have been transformed.

In both cases, the story begins in a river valley: that of the Skeena, that of the Nass. It is winter, and famine reigns. Two related women, one living upstream and the other downstream, decide to join forces, and meet half-way.

Already, several differences are apparent:

Place of the Action	Nass	Skeena
State of the River	?	Frozen

Situation of the Two Villages	Not far apart	'Very far apart'[20]
Relationship between the Two Women	Sisters	Mother and daughter
Civil Status	$\left\{\begin{array}{l}\text{1 married} \\ \text{1 unmarried}\end{array}\right\}$	2 widows

These differences, it is clear, are equivalent to a *weakening of all the oppositions* in the Nass version. This is very striking in the (contrasted) situations of the two villages and even more so in the (contrasted) relationships between the two women. In the latter there is a constant element, the relationship of elder to younger, which is manifested in the form: *mother/ daughter* in the one case, and *elder sister/younger sister* in the other, the first couple living *farther apart* from one another than the second and being brought together by a *more radical event* (the double simultaneous widowhood) than the second (of whom only one is married – it is not stated whether she has lost her husband).

One may also prove that the Nass version is a weakening of the Skeena version and that the Skeena version is not a strengthened form of the other. The proof lies in the vestigial survival of the original mother/daughter relationship in the form of the maternity of the elder sister, who is accompanied by her daughter, a detail which in every other respect has no function in the Nass version:

(*a*) [mother : daughter] :: [(mother + daughter) : non-mother]
the constant element being given by the opposition between *retrospective fertility* and *prospective fertility*.

But these differences, which one could consider as being 'more' or 'less', and in this sense quantitative, are accompanied by others which are genuine inversions.

In the Skeena version, the elder of the two women comes from down-river, the younger from up-river. In the Nass variant, the contrary is true, since the pair (mother + daughter) comes from Gitwunksilk, upstream of the Canyon, and the unmarried sister (who will marry the supernatural protector and is therefore identical with the daughter in the Skeena version) arrives from Laxqaltsap, which is downstream.

In the Skeena version, the women are completely empty-

handed, reduced to sharing *a single rotten berry*, found at their
meeting-place ('a few berries' in Boas, 1895). Once again, the
Nass version shows a weakening, since the women bring
provisions, though they are in fact very meagre: a handful of
berries and a piece of spawn:

	Down-river	*Up-river*
Skeena version:	0———→rotten←———0	
	berry	
Nass version:	berries———→	←———spawn

It would be easy to show that on the Northwest Pacific Coast
and in other regions of America, decomposition is considered as
the borderline between food and excrement.[21] If, in the Skeena
version, a single berry (*quantatively*, the minimal food) is the
bearer of decomposition (*qualitatively*, the minimal food), then
it is because berries in themselves are thought of *specifically* as
a weak kind of food, in contrast with strong foods.

Without any doubt, in the Skeena version the two women are
deliberately associated not with any particular food, but with
the lack of any sort of food. This 'dearth of food' however,
though a negative category, is not an empty category, for the
development of the myth gives it, in retrospect, a content.
The two women represent 'absence of food', but they are also
bound respectively to the East and to the West, to the land
and to the sea. The myth of Asdiwal tells of an opposition
between two types of life, also bound up with the same cardinal
points and the same elements: mountain-hunters on the one
side, fishermen and sea-hunters on the other (Boas, 1916,
p. 403: 'The sea-hunter required a training quite different from
that of the mountain-hunter'). In the Skeena version the
'alimentary' opposition is therefore double: (1) between animal
food (at the extreme positions) and vegetable food (in the
intermediate position) and (2) between sea-animal (West) and
land-animal (East), thus:

Vegetable food:	middle	not defined[22]
	↑	(*non-marqué*)
	(1)	
	↓	
Animal food:	$\frac{(sea)}{(West)}$ ←— (2)—→ $\frac{(land)}{(East)}$	strongly defined[22]
		(*marqué*)

36

From this we obtain the formula:

(*b*) [land : sea] :: [(sea + land) : middle]

and the analogy of this with (*a*) [p. 35] is immediately obvious.

The alimentary system of the Nass version is based on a *simplified structure* (with two terms instead of three) and on *weakened oppositions*. From being 'not-defined', vegetable food moves to a state of being 'weakly defined'; from a borderline state between 'food' and 'absence of food', it becomes a positive food, both quantitatively (a handful of berries) and qualitatively (fresh berries). This vegetable food is now opposed not to animal food as such, a category which is strongly defined (and here distinguished by a minus sign (-1)), but to the weakest imaginable manifestation of this same animal food (to which we still assign a plus sign ($+1$)). This contrast between 'weakly defined animal food' and 'strongly defined animal food' is exhibited in three ways:

> fish and not meat
> fish spawn and not fish
> a piece 'as big as the finger'

Thus we have a system:

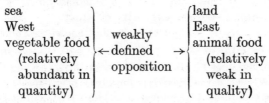

From the point of view of the alimentary system, the correlation between the two variants of the myth can thus be expressed by the following formulae:

(c_1) [($-$meat) : ($-$fish)] :: [dx(meat + fish) : dx(vegetable food)]

or in simplified form (ignoring the minute quantity dx):

(c_2) [meat : fish] :: [(meat + fish) : (vegetable food)]

where the sum of (meat + fish) constitutes the category of animal food. It will be noticed, once again, that there is an analogy between the three formulae *a*, *b*, and *c*.

The two types of food in the Nass version are berries (down-stream) and spawn (upstream). Spawn is an animal food from the river, berries a vegetable food from the land (earth), and, of all earth-grown foods, this (in contrast to the game that is hunted in the mountains) is the one most commonly associated with the river banks (Boas, 1916, p. 404: 'Women go out jointly by canoe or walking in the woods to gather berries').

Thus the transformation which has occurred in the process of transferring the story from the one version to the other can, from this point of view, be written as follows:

(d) [West : East] :: [sea : land] :: [water : land (earth)]
    :: [river : bank]

But the opposition between the river and its banks is not only a weakened form of the fundamental contrasts between 'East' and 'West' and between 'land (earth)' and 'water', which are most strongly defined in the opposition: sea/land. It is also a *function* of this last opposition.

In fact, the opposition river/bank is more strongly defined inland (where the element 'water' is reduced to 'river') than towards the coast. There the opposition is no longer so pertinent because, in the category 'water', the sea takes precedence over the river, and in the category 'land (earth)', the coast takes precedence over the bank. One can thus understand the logic of the reversal whereby, *up-river*, we are led to put:

(d) [water : land (earth)] :: [river : bank]

whereas *down-river* – when the whole of the river and its banks are assimilated into the category 'land,' this time in opposition to the category 'sea' – we are led to write:

(e) [water : land (earth)] :: [sea : (river + bank)]

where the combination (river + bank) has, by permutation, been moved into the position originally occupied by 'land'.

Since (d) and (e) can be recast in the form:

(f) [land : water] :: [(river + bank) : sea]

which is analogous to formulae (a), (b), and (c), this example shows how a mythological transformation can be expressed by a series of equivalences, such that the two extremes are radically inverted (cf. Lévi-Strauss, 1963a, pp. 228-229).

In fact, in the last stage of the transformation, the (downstream, West) position is occupied by a vegetable food, that is to say by an 'earth-food', while the (upstream, East) position is occupied by an animal food, which, since it consists of fish-spawn, comes from the river and is therefore a 'water-food'.

The two women, reduced to their common denominator, which is the relationship older/younger, have thus, in coherent fashion, had their positions changed over with respect to the relationship upstream/downstream.[23]

Consequently, in the Skeena version, the weak opposition between river and bank is *neutralized* (this is expressed in the myth by specifying that the river is frozen and that the women walk on the ice) in favour of the strong opposition between sea and land which is, however, negatively evoked (since the women are defined by their lack of the foods which are associated with their respective (territorial) positions). In the Nass version it is the strong opposition which is neutralized, by weakening and inversion, in favour of the weak opposition between river and bank, which is positively evoked (since in this case the women are provided, albeit meagrely, with the appropriate foods).

Parallel transformations are to be found in the episode of the supernatural protector as related by the two versions. In that of the Skeena, he provides meat alone, in an ever-increasing quantity (in order: little squirrel, grouse, porcupine, beaver, goat, black bear, grizzly bear, caribou); in the Nass version, he provides meat and fish at the same time in such large quantities that in the one case the hut is 'full of meat and fish' but only 'full of dried meat' in the other. In the Skeena version this balance between the two types of life is brought about only much later and in a transitory way: during Asdiwal's third marriage with the sister of the Gitxatla people, when, accompanied by his brothers-in-law, he is abundantly provided with 'salmon and fresh meat' which he sells to the starving Tsimshian (cf. Boas, 1902, pp. 225-226, and Boas, 1912, pp. 74-77 and 120-123).

On the other hand, Asdiwal's father gives him magic objects which are immediately effective (Skeena version), whereas those given to Asi-hwil have to be gradually perfected (Nass version). In each case, the hero returns from the West like the food, transported in the insides of a sea-lion; but in the second case the change from stomach (Skeena) to intestines (Nass) suggests a food that is nearer to putrefaction, a theme that is final here and no longer initial (a rotten berry and rotten bark

were the women's first food in the Skeena version). Nor must it
be forgotten that, from this point of view, the candlefish, the
only hope of escaping from starvation (in Tsimshian, candlefish
is called: *hale-mâ'tk*, which means 'saviour') must be tolerated
up to the point of decomposition – otherwise the fish would be
offended and would never return.

IX

How can a concrete content be given to this double mechanism
of the *weakening of oppositions*, accompanied by a *reversal of
correlations* the formal coherence of which we have now
established? It should first be noted that the inversion is given
in the respective geographical positions of the two populations:
the Nisqa, people of the Nass, are found in the North; the
Tsimshian (whose name means: 'inside the river Skeena' from
K-sia'n: 'Skeena') in the South. In order to marry on (relatively
speaking) foreign territory, the Nass hero goes to the land of
the Tsimshian, that is to say, towards the Skeena, in the
South; and the Skeena-born Asdiwal's last marriage shows him,
up to the time of the break, camping with his in-laws on the
Nass and thus in the North. Each population spontaneously
forms symmetrical but inverse conceptions of the same country.

But the myths bear witness to the fact that the duality:
Skeena valley/Nass valley, which, with the region in between,
forms the Tsimshian country (in the broadest sense) is seen as
an opposition, as are also the economic activities which are
respectively associated with each of the two rivers:

A young man of miraculous birth decided to go up to heaven
while night reigned on earth. Changed into a leaf, he impreg-
nated the daughter of the Master of the Sun, who bore a son
called Giant. The child seized the sun, made himself master of
daylight and went down to earth where he found himself a
companion, Logobola, who was master of mist, water, and
marshes. The two boys had a competition, and after several
undecided contests they decided to shoot arrows and play
for the River Skeena against the River Nass. Giant won by
a trick and was so overjoyed that he spoke in Tsimshian – in

the dialect of the lower reaches of the Skeena – to voice his feelings 'And Logobola says: "You won, Brother Giant. Now the candlefish will come to Nass River twice every summer." And Txamsem (Giant) said, "And the salmon of Skeena River shall always be fat." Thus they divided what Txamsem had won at Nass river. . . . After which the two brothers parted.' One of the versions recorded by Boas says: 'Txamsem went down to the ocean and Logobola went southward to the place he had come from' (Boas, 1916, p. 70. Cf. also Boas, 1902, p. 7ff.).

In any case, the symmetry of the geographical positions provides only the beginning of an explanation. We have seen that the reversal of correlations is itself the function of a general weakening of all the oppositions which cannot be explained merely by a substitution of South for North and North for South. In passing from the Skeena to the Nass, the myth becomes distorted in two ways, which are structurally connected: first, it is reduced and, second, it is reversed. In order to be admissible, any interpretation must take account of both of these aspects.

The Skeena people and the Nass people speak similar dialects (Boas, 1911). Their social organization is almost identical.[24] But their modes of life are profoundly different. We have described the way of life on the Skeena and on the coast, characterized by a great seasonal movement which is in fact two-phased: between the winter towns and the spring camps on one hand, and then between the spring candlefish season on the Nass and the summer salmon-fishing on the Skeena.

As for the Nass people, it does not seem that they made periodic visits to the Skeena. The most that we are told is that those who lived very far up the Nass were called 'kit'anwi'likc', 'people who left their permanent villages from time to time', because they came down towards the Nass estuary each year, but only for the candlefish season (Sapir, 1915, p. 3). The largest seasonal migrations of the Nisqa seem thus to have been limited to the Nass, while those of the Tsimshian were based on a much more complex Skeena-Nass system. The reason is that the candlefish only visit the Nass, which therefore becomes the meeting-place of all the groups who anxiously await the arrival of their 'saviour', whereas the salmon goes up both rivers indiscriminately. Thus the Nisqa lived in one valley, and the Tsimshian in two.

Since this is so, all the natives are able to conceptualize the duality Nass/Skeena as an opposition which correlates with that of candlefish/salmon. There can be no doubt about it, since the myth which lays the foundation of this opposition was recorded by Boas in two practically identical versions, one in Nass dialect, the other in Skeena dialect. But an opposition which is recognized by all need not have the same significance for each group. The Tsimshian lived through this opposition in the course of each year; the Nisqa were content to know about it. Although a grammatical construction employing couplets of antithetical terms is present in the Tsimshian tongue as a very obvious model, and probably presents itself as such quite consciously to the speaker,[25] its logical and philosophical implication would not be the same in each of the two groups. The Tsimshian use it to build up a system which is global and coherent but which is not communicable in its entirety to people whose concrete experiences are not stamped with the same duality; perhaps, also, the fact that the course of the Nass is less definitely orientated from East to West than is that of the Skeena adds to the obscurity of the topographical schema (among the Nisqa).

Thus we arrive at a fundamental property of mythical thought, other examples of which might well be sought elsewhere. When a mythical schema is transmitted from one population to another, and there exist differences of language, social organization or way of life which make the myth difficult to communicate, it begins to become impoverished and confused. But one can find a limiting situation in which instead of being finally obliterated by losing all its outlines, the myth is inverted and regains part of its precision.

Similar inversions occur in optics. An image can be seen in full detail when observed through any adequately large aperture. But as the aperture is narrowed the image becomes blurred and difficult to see. When, however, the aperture is further reduced to a pinpoint, that is to say, when *communica-*

tion is about to vanish, the image is inverted and becomes clear again. This experiment is used in schools to demonstrate the propagation of light in straight lines, or in other words to prove that rays of light are not transmitted at random, but within the limits of a structured field.

This study is in its own way an experiment, since it is limited to a single case, and the elements isolated by analysis appear in several series of concomitant variations. If the experiment has helped to demonstrate that the field of mythical thought, too, is structured, then it will have achieved its object.

NOTES

1. The candlefish (*olachen*) is a small very oily fish caught in very large numbers. Valued mainly for its oil, the meat can be eaten in times of scarcity [E.R.L.].

2. Hatsenas (Boas, 1912), Hadsenas (Boas, 1895): it is a bird like the robin but not a robin (Boas, 1912, pp. 72-73). In another myth the robin announces the summer (cf. Boas, 1912, pp. 200-201). The term 'robin' is applied to a variety of birds by the English and the Americans. It would be rash to try to identify the species. According to Boas (1895), Hadsenas means 'luck', and describes a bird sent as a messenger from Heaven (p. 286).

In this work, which has no linguistic pretentions, the transcription of native terms has been simplified to the extreme, keeping only those distinctions which are essential for avoiding ambiguities between the terms quoted.

3. The name Asdiwal certainly has several connotations. The Nass form, Asi-hwil, means 'Crosser of Mountains' (Boas, 1902, p. 226) but cf. also '*asdiwal*', 'to be in danger' (Boas, 1912, Glossary, p. 257) and Asewaelgyet: a different name for and special variety of the Thunder Bird (Barbeau, 1950, Vol. I, pp. 144-145 and Vol. II, p. 476).

4. For a summary and comparative analysis of all the texts which have been listed as referring to the greed of the Demiurge, see Boas (1916, p. 636 ff.).

5. As the smallest mammal to appear in mythology, and also because in the mythology of the Northwest Coast the mouse represents the animals of the earth at their most modest level: that of domestic life. The mouse is in fact the domestic animal of the earth. With this distinction she is entitled to the tiny offering of fat which drips from woollen ear-ornaments when they are thrown into the fire in her honour.

6. 'The love of the master of the sea-lions and of his whole tribe increased very much' (Boas, 1912, p. 133).

7. The Tsimshian of the Nisqa group 'look to the river [Nass] for their food supply, which consists principally of salmon and candlefish. Indeed it is owing to the enormous numbers of the latter fish that run in to spawn in the early spring that the name Nass, meaning "the stomach, or food depot" has been given to the river' (G. T. Emmons, 1910).

8. In Lévi-Strauss's writings the notion of a structured conceptual scheme (*schème conceptuel*), which lies at the back of explicit cultural forms and

consists in the main of elements linked in binary opposition, is of basic importance. See, in particular *La Pensée sauvage* (1962b, p. 173). Throughout this translation the French *schème* has been consistently rendered as English 'schema' and French *opposition* as English 'opposition' even though in places it might have been more elegant to write 'framework' or 'setting' for *schème*, and 'contrast' or 'antithesis' for *opposition* [E.R.L.].

9. As we shall see later, the apparent gap in the cycle is explained by the fact that in the story of Waux, Asdiwal's son, the closure will be the result of a matrilateral marriage which ends in a terminal situation: husband and wife without children.

10. Asdiwal himself had inherited from his father the lightness and speed of a bird, qualities which are ideally suited to a hunter who, according to native thought, should be as light-footed as a bird on the wing (Boas, 1916, p. 403). Boas's informant considers Waux as Asdiwal's only child (Boas, 1916, p. 243). This is a mistake, for Asdiwal also had a son by his third marriage (Boas, 1912, pp. 123, 133, 135). But this point is unimportant since the third marriage was simply a doublet of the second.

11. Boas's informant seems to have made a mistake which Boas has only partially corrected. In Boas (1916) the text is as follows 'Before his mother died she wanted her son to marry one of her own cousins, and he did what his mother wanted him to do' (p. 244). Thus it would be a cousin of the mother and not of the son. The corresponding native text is to be found in Durlach (1928, p. 124) of which herewith a transcription (in simplified signs): na gauga(?) dem dzake na'ot da hasa'x a dem naksde lguolget a k!âlda lgu-txaât. . . .

The kinship term *txaâ* denotes the father's sister's or the mother's brother's children – that is to say, all cross-cousins. *Lgu-* is a diminutive. The suffix *-t* is a third person possessive. In his summary of the story of Waux, Boas repeats the suspect phrase: 'He marries one of his mother's cousins' (Boas, 1916, p. 825). But in the commentary he corrects his interpretation by placing this example quite rightly with all those he quotes of marriages with a matrilateral cross-cousin. 'The normal type of marriage, as described in the traditions, is that between a young man and his mother's brother's daughter. Thus . . . a mother requests her daughter to marry her cousin (244)' (Boas, 1916, p. 440). Since p. 244 only mentions Waux's marriage, it is clear that this time Boas rectifies the kinship relations, but confuses the sex of the husband and wife. From this there arises a new contradiction, for this cousin would be the father's sister's daughter. The real meaning seems to be: before dying, his mother wanted him to marry one of his own cousins.

12. Boas (1916, pp. 185-191): Describing the marriage ceremonies of the Nisqa as reported by another informant, Boas explains that the fight between the two groups can become so violent that one of the slaves in the suitor's guard is killed: 'This foretells that the couple will never part' (Boas, 1916, p. 531).

13. Boas (1916, p. 403). Asdiwal's double visit to heaven (which contrasts with his single journey below the earth) seems to be intended to make even clearer the analogy with salmon-fishing. In fact, his return to heaven takes place exactly as if it were a 'catch', in a net which is let down through an opening in the heavens: just like the ritual fishing for the first salmon of spring, which is carried out with a net, through a hole made in the ice which still covers the river.

14. Boas (1912, pp. 112-113). If our interpretation is correct, it must be

admitted that the explicit opposition: sky/earth is here realized in an implicit form: sky/water, which is the strongest opposition inherent in the system of the three elements as used by the myth.

This system can in fact be represented by the following formula (read the sign : to mean 'is to', the sign :: to mean 'as', the sign > to mean 'is above', and the sign / to mean 'is opposed to')

1. sky : earth :: earth : water

which can also be written

2. sky > earth > water

Then the hypothesis put forward above about the 'fishing up' of Asdiwal can be verified by the following permutation:

3. sky : water :: earth : earth

which may be said to correspond to Asdiwal's second supernatural voyage, where the opposition to water (earth) is expressed by a subterranean voyage. We are therefore perfectly entitled to put

4. sky/earth :: sky/water (where 'water' stands for 'beneath the sky')

5. earth/water :: earth/earth (where '/earth' stands for 'below the ground')

But this duplication of the 'earth' pole is only made necessary by the assimilation (in veiled terms) of the major opposition between sky and earth to the minor opposition, still implicit, between earth and water: Asdiwal is fished up like a fish off an earth which is confused with the liquid element, from the heights of a sky pictured in terrestial terms as a 'green and fertile prairie'.

From the very beginning the myth seems governed by one particular opposition which is more vital than the others, even if not immediately perceptible: that between earth and water, which is also the one most closely linked with methods of production and the objective relationships between men and the world. Formal though it be, analysis of a society's myths verifies the primacy of the infrastructures.

15. See Boas's hesitations in Boas (1916, pp. 401, 411, 412). Even Garfield, who gave the problems much attention, cannot bring herself to admit to the existence of succession in the paternal line. See Garfield, Wingert & Barbeau (1951, p. 17).

16. Boas (1916, p. 793). None the less, there are a few minor differences which suggest that Boas (1895) is a weak variant of Boas (1912).

17. J. R. Swanton (1952). 'Lakkulzap or Greenville' (p. 586); 'Gitwinksilk . . . near the mouth of Nass River' (*idem*). In any case, Barbeau's map (1950) places Gitwinksilk (Gitwinksihlt) upstream of the Canyon.

18. E. Sapir (1915): 'Greenville (laxqaltsa'p) . . .' (p. 2). According to Sapir, the Gitwankcitlku, 'people of the place where lizards live', from the third Nisqa group, starting from downstream.

19. Sapir (1915): 'Gitxate'n, people of the fish traps' (p. 3). Barbeau (1950, map) Gitrhatin, at the mouth of the estuary and downstream from the canyon.

20. That is, at any rate, what the myth emphatically affirms – but the village of the younger woman is not named.

21. Many myths treat of the loss of salmon by mankind, thanks to men's refusing a piece of mouldy fish, or to their disgust on discovering that the Mother of Salmon gives birth by her excretory canal.

22. Lévi-Strauss's distinction *marqué/non-mraqué* is here rendered 'defined'/ 'not defined', but note also the distinction 'marked'/'unmarked' as it occurs in general linguistics. In the latter context the words *man* and *author* are 'unmarked' in comparison with the words *woman* and *authoress* which are

'marked'. Here the 'unmarked' term will be presumed to include the 'marked' category unless the latter is explicitly distinguished. For a full discussion, see Greenberg (1966).

23. The younger woman, representing prospective fertility, shows a markedly feminine character; in the elder this is not so marked. The younger must always be in the (earth) position: in the Skeena version, because she is to bear Asdiwal, master of mountains and earth-born hunter; in the Nass version for the same reason, and also because of the strictly feminine character of the gatherer of berries, which stand for earth-food. Cf. Boas (1916): 'while the men procure all the animal food except shellfish, the women gather berries and dig roots and shellfish' (p. 52, also p. 404).

24. E. Sapir (1915, pp. 3-7), where it is clear that Goddard (1934) was wrong in attributing only two exogamic divisions to the Nisqa instead of four. This mistake can probably be explained by the fact that the Nisqa, immediate neighbours of the Tlingit, find it necessary more often than the Tsimshian to apply the rule of the lowest common multiple to their social organization, so that the laws of exogamy may be respected in marriages with foreigners.

25. Boas quotes 31 pairs of 'local particles' in oppositions of the following type: up along the ground–down along the ground; up through the air–down through the air; into–out of; backwards–forwards, etc. (Boas, 1911, pp. 300-312).

REFERENCES

BARBEAU, M. 1950. Totem Poles. *National Museum of Canada Bulletin*, No. 119, Anthropological Series No. 30.

BEYNON, W. 1941. The Tsimshians of Metlakatla. *American Anthropologist* **43**: 83-88.

BOAS, FRANZ. 1895. *Indianische Sagen von der Nord-Pacifischen Küste Amerikas*. Berlin.

—— 1902. Tsimshian Texts. *Bulletin of Smithsonian Institution*, No. 27. Bureau of American Ethnology, Washington.

—— 1911. 'Tsimshian' in *Handbook of American Indian Languages*, Part I. Smithsonian Institution, Bureau of American Ethnology, Bulletin 40, Part I.

—— 1912. *Tsimshian Texts (New Series)*. Publication of American Ethnological Society, Vol. III. Leyden.

—— 1916. *Tsimshian Mythology*. Annual Report Smithsonian Institution, No. 31 (1909-1910). Washington: Bureau of American Ethnology.

DURLACH, T. M. 1928. *The Relationship Systems of the Tlingit, Haida and Tsimshian*. Publications of American Ethnological Society, Vol. XI. New York.

EMMONS, G. T. 1910. 'Niska' in *Handbook of American Indians North of Mexico*. Smithsonian Institution, Bureau of American Ethnology, Bulletin 30, Part II.

GARFIELD, V. E. 1939. *Tsimshian Clan and Society*. University of Washington Publications in Anthropology, Vol. 7, No. 3.

GARFIELD, V. E., WINGERT, P. S. & BARBEAU, M. 1951. *The Tsimshian: Their Arts and Music.* Publications of American Ethnological Society, Vol. XVIII. New York.

GODDARD, P. E. 1934. *Indians of the Northwest Coast.* American Museum of Natural History, Handbook Series No. 10. New York.

GREENBERG, J. H. 1966. Language Universals. In T. A. Sebeok (ed.), *Current Trends in Linguistics,* Volume 3: *Theoretical Foundations.* The Hague: Mouton, pp. 62ff.

LÉVI-STRAUSS, C. 1949. *Les Structures élémentaires de la parenté.* Paris: Presses Universitaires de France.

—— 1958a. *Anthropologie structurale.* Paris: Plon (English translation, 1963a. *Structural Anthropology.* New York: Basic Books).

—— 1962b. *La Pensée sauvage.* Paris: Plon.

MALINOWSKI, B. 1932. *The Sexual Life of Savages in North-Western Melanesia,* 3rd edn. London: Routledge.

RICHARDS, J. F. 1914. Cross Cousin Marriage in South India. *Man* 14.

SAPIR, E. 1915. A Sketch of the Social Organisation of the Nass River Indians. *Museum Bulletin of the Canadian Dept. of Mines, Geological Survey,* No. XIX. Ottawa.

SWANTON, J. R. 1909. *Contributions to the Ethnology of the Haida.* Memoirs of American Museum of Natural History, Vol. VIII.

—— 1952. *The Indian Tribes of North America.* Smithsonian Institution, Bureau of American Ethnology, Bulletin 145.

WEDGEWOOD, C. H. 1928. Cousin Marriage in *Encyclopaedia Britannica,* 14th edn.

Mary Douglas

The Meaning of Myth

With special reference to 'La Geste d'Asdiwal'

Social anthropology, as we know it, was born of a professedly empirical approach. And it was first developed in Britain. These two marks, of being British and empirical, are not accidentally linked. This is the home of philosophical scepticism, an attitude of thought which has insulated us more effectively than the North Sea and the Channel from Continental movements of ideas. Our intellectual climate is plodding and anti-metaphysical. Yet, in spite of these traditions, we cannot read much of Lévi-Strauss without feeling some excitement. To social studies he holds out a promise of the sudden lift that new methods of science could give. He has developed his vision so elaborately and documented it so massively from so many fields of our subject that he commands our attention.

He has developed most explicitly in connection with myth his ideas of the place of sociology within a single grand discipline of Communication. This part of his teaching draws very broadly on the structural analysis of linguistics, and on cybernetics and communication theory in general, and to some extent on the related theory of games. Briefly, its starting-point is that it is the nature of the mind to work through form. Any experience is received in a structured form, and these forms or structures, which are a condition of knowing, are generally unconscious (as, for example, unconscious categories of language). Furthermore, they vary little in modern or in ancient times. They always consist in the creation of pairs of opposites, which are balanced against one another and built up in various (algebraically representable) ways. All the different kinds of patterned activity can be analysed according to the different structures they produce. For example, social life is a matter of interaction between persons. There are three different types of social communication. First, there is kinship, the structure underlying the rules for transferring women; second, there is the economy, that is the structure underlying transfer of goods and services; third, there is the underlying structure of language. The promise is that if we can get at these structures, display and compare them, the way is open for a true science of society, so far a will-o'-the-wisp for sociologists.

So far myth has not been mentioned. Lévi-Strauss recognizes that its structures belong to a different level of mental activity from those of language, and the technique of analysis must be correspondingly different. The technique is described in his 'Structural Study of Myth' (1955) and is also made very clear in Edmund Leach's two articles (1961, 1962) in which he applies the technique to the Book of Genesis. It assumes that the analysis of myth should proceed like the analysis of language. In both language and myth the separate units have no meaning by themselves, they acquire it only because of the way in which they are combined. The best comparison is with musical notation: there is no musical meaning in a single isolated note. Describing the new science of mythologics which is to parallel linguistics, Lévi-Strauss unguardedly says that the units of mythological structure are sentences. If he took this statement seriously it would be an absurd limitation on analysis. But in fact, quite rightly, he abandons it at once, making great play with the structure underlying the meaning of a set of names. What are sentences, anyway? Linguists would be at a loss to identify these units of language structure which Lévi-Strauss claims to be able to put on punched cards and into a computing machine as surely and simply as if they were phonemes and morphemes. For me and for most of us, computer talk is a mysterious language very apt for prestidigitation. Does he really mean that he can chop a myth into semantic units, put them through a machine, and get out at the other end an underlying pattern which is not precisely the one he used for selecting his units? The quickness of the hand deceives the eye. Does he further believe that this underlying structure is the real meaning or sense of the myth? He says that it is the deepest kind of sense, more important than the uninitiated reader would suspect. However, I do not think it is fair to such an ebullient writer to take him literally. In other contexts it is plain that

Lévi-Strauss realizes that any myth has multiple meanings and
that no one of them can be labelled the deepest or the truest.
More of this later.

From the point of view of anthropology, one of his novel
departures is to treat all versions of a myth as equally authentic
or relevant. This is right, of course. Linguistic analysis can be
applied to any literary unit, and the longer the better, so long
as there is real unity underlying the stretches of language that
are analysed together. Why stop short at one of Shakespeare's
historical plays? Why not include the whole of Shakespeare?
Or the whole of Elizabethan drama? Here Lévi-Strauss gives
one of his disturbing twists of thought that make the plodding
reader uneasily suspect that he is being duped. For by 'version'
we find that Lévi-Strauss means both version and interpretation.
He insists that Freud's treatment of the Oedipus myth must
be put through the machine together with other earlier versions.
This challenging idea is not merely for the fun of shocking the
bourgeois mythologist out of his search for original versions.
Freud used the Oedipus myth to stand for his own discovery
that humans are each individually concerned with precisely the
problem of 'birth from one' or 'birth from two' parents. On
Lévi-Strauss's analysis of its structure, this problem is revealed
as underlying the Oedipus cycle. So there is no inconsistency
between Freud and Sophocles. But the reference to Freud
interestingly vindicates Lévi-Strauss on a separate charge.
Some must feel that the themes which his technique reveals
are too trivial and childish either to have been worth the
excavation, or to have been worth the erecting of an elaborate
myth series in the first place. But after Freud no one can be
sure that an individual's speculation about his own genesis is a
trivial puzzle without emotional force.

I admit that the use of all interpretations of a great myth
might not always so triumphantly vindicate this method.
Meyer Fortes (1959) treated Oedipus rather differently in
Oedipus and Job in West Africa. Compare St Augustine, Simone
Weil (1950), and Edmund Leach (1962) on the Biblical story of
Noah drunk in the vineyard: for one the drunken, naked Noah
is Christ humiliated; for the other he is the dionysian mysteries
too austerely rejected by the Jewish priesthood, and for the

last the tale is a trite lesson about Hebrew sexual morality. I will say more below of how these 'versions' would look coming out of the mythologic computer. At this stage of the discussion we should treat the computer as a red herring and forget for the moment the quest for the real meaning. We can then begin seriously to evaluate Lévi-Strauss's approach to mythology.

First, we should recognize his debt to the dialectical method of Hegelian-Marxist philosophy. The dialectic was Hegel's speculation about the nature of reality and about the logical technique by which it could be grasped. When Lévi-Strauss says that mythic thought follows a strict logic of its own, he means a Hegelian logic of thesis, antithesis, and synthesis, moving in ever more complex cycles to comprehend all the oppositions and limitations inherent in thought. According to Lévi-Strauss, the structure of myth is a dialectic structure in which opposed logical positions are stated, the oppositions mediated by a restatement, which again, when its internal structure becomes clear, gives rise to another kind of opposition, which in its turn is mediated or resolved, and so on.

On the assumption that it is the nature of myth to mediate contradictions, the method of analysis must proceed by distinguishing the oppositions and the mediating elements. And it follows, too, that the function of myth is to portray the contradictions in the basic premises of the culture. The same goes for the relation of myth to social reality. The myth is a contemplation of the unsatisfactory compromises which, after all, compose social life. In the devious statements of the myth, people can recognize· indirectly what it would be difficult to admit openly and yet what is patently clear to all and sundry, that the ideal is not attainable.

Lévi-Strauss does not stick his neck out so far as to say that people are reconciled better or worse to their makeshift arrangements and contradictory formulae – but merely that myth makes explicit their experience of the contradictoriness of reality.

A summary of 'La Geste d'Asdiwal'[1] best demonstrates how this is to be understood. It is a cycle of myths told by the Tsimshian tribes. These are a sparse population of migratory hunters and fishers who live on the Pacific coast, south of Alaska. They are culturally in the same group with Haida and

Tlingit, northernmost representatives of Northwest Coast culture. Topographically their territory is dominated by the two parallel rivers, Nass and Skeena, which flow southwest to the sea. In the summer they live on vegetable products collected by women, and in winter on marine and land animals and fish killed by the men. The movements of fish and game dictate their seasonal movements between sea and mountains, and the northern and southern rivers. The Tsimshian were organized in dispersed matrilineal clans and lived in typical Northwest Coast composite dwellings which housed several families. They tended to live with their close maternal kin, generally practising avunculocal residence at marriage and the ideal was to marry a mother's brother's daughter.

The myth begins during the winter famine in the Skeena valley. A mother and daughter, separated hitherto by their marriages but now both widowed by the famine, set out from East and West, one from upstream and one from downstream of the frozen Skeena, to meet each other half-way. The daughter becomes the wife of a mysterious bird who feeds them both and when she gives birth to a miraculous child, Asdiwal, its bird father gives him a magic bow and arrow, lance, snow-shoes, cloak, and hat which make him invisible at will, invincible, and able to produce an inexhaustible supply of food. The old mother dies and the bird father disappears. Asdiwal and his mother walk West to her natal village. From there he follows a white bear into the sky where it is revealed as Evening-Star, the daughter of the Sun. When Asdiwal has succeeded, thanks to his magic equipment, in a series of impossible tasks, the Sun allows him to marry Evening-Star, and, because he is homesick, to take his wife back to the earth generously supplied with magic food. On earth, because Asdiwal is unfaithful to her, his sky wife leaves him. He follows her half-way to the sky, where she kills him with a thunderbolt. His father-in-law, the Sun, brings him to life and they live together in the sky until Asdiwal feels homesick again. Once home, Asdiwal finds his mother is dead and, since nothing keeps him in her village, he continues walking to the West. This time he makes a

Tsimshian marriage, which starts off well, Asdiwal using his magic hunting-weapons to good effect. In the spring he, his wife, and her four brothers move along the coast northwards, towards the River Nass, but Asdiwal challenges his brothers-in-law to prove that their sea-hunting is better than his land-hunting. Asdiwal wins the contest by bringing home four dead bears from his mountain hunt, one for each of the four brothers, who return empty handed from their sea expedition. Furious at their defeat, they carry off their sister and abandon Asdiwal, who then joins some strangers also going North towards the Nass for the candlefish season. Once again, there are four brothers, and a sister whom Asdiwal marries. After a good fishing season, Asdiwal returns with his in-laws and wife to their village, where his wife bears them a son. One day, however, he boasts that he is better than his brothers-in-law at walrus-hunting. Put to the test, he succeeds brilliantly, again infuriating his wife's brothers, who abandon him without food or fire to die on a rocky reef. His bird father preserves him through a raging storm. Finally, he is taken by a mouse to the underground home of the walruses whom he has wounded. Asdiwal cures them and asks in exchange a safe return. The King of the Walruses lends Asdiwal his stomach as a boat, on which he sails home. There he finds his faithful wife, who helps him to kill her own brothers. But again Asdiwal, assailed by homesickness, leaves his wife and returns to the Skeena valley, where his son joins him. When winter comes, Asdiwal goes hunting in the mountains, but forgetting his snow-shoes, can go neither up nor down and is changed into stone.

This is the end of the story. In the analysis which follows, Lévi-Strauss draws out the remarkably complex symmetry of different levels of structure. Asdiwal's journeys take him from East to West, then North to the Nass, then Southwest to the sea fishing of walrus, and finally Southeast back to the Skeena River. So the points of the compass and the salient points of order of Tsimshian migration are laid out. This is the geographical sequence. There is another sequence concerned with residence at marriage, as follows.

The two women who open the tale have been separated by
the daughter's virilocal residence at marriage. Living together,
they set up what Lévi-Strauss calls a 'matrilocal residence of
the simplest kind, mother and daughter'. Lévi-Strauss counts
the first marriage of the bird father of Asdiwal as matrilocal.
Then the sky marriage of Asdiwal himself with Evening-Star is
counted as matrilocal, and matrilocal again the two human
marriages of Asdiwal, until after he has come back from the
walrus kingdom, when his wife betrays her brothers. So,
Lévi-Strauss remarks that all the marriages of Asdiwal are
matrilocal until the end. Then the regular pattern is inverted
and 'patrilocalism triumphs' because Asdiwal abandons his wife
and goes home, accompanied by his son. The story starts with
the reunion of a mother and daughter, liberated from their
spouses (and paternal kin in the case of the daughter), and ends
with the reunion of a father and son, liberated from their spouses
(and maternal kin in the case of the son). To the English
anthropologist some of this symmetry and inversion seems
rather far-fetched. The evidence for counting the bird marriage
as matrilocal is dubious and the sky marriage is plain groom
service. The rejection of the third wife is hardly 'patrilocalism'.
But more about inversion below. I want to go into details of
another sociological sequence which produces two more pairs of
oppositions which are also inverted at the end.

The same symmetry is traced in the cosmological sequence.
First, the hero sojourns in the sky where he is wounded and
cured by the sky people; then he makes an underground sojourn
where he finds underground people whom *he* has wounded, and
whom *he* cures. There is a similar elaboration of recurring
themes of famine and plenty. They correspond faithfully enough
to the economic reality of Tsimshian life. Using his knowledge
of another myth of the region, Lévi-Strauss explains their
implication. The Northwest Coast Indians attribute the present
condition of the world to the disturbances made by a great
Crow, whose voracious appetite initiated all the processes of
creation. So hunger is the condition of movement, glut is a static
condition. The first phase of the Asdiwal tale opposes Sky and
Earth, the Sun and the earthly human. These oppositions the
hero overcomes, thanks to his bird father. But Asdiwal breaks

the harmony established between these elements: first he feels homesick, then, once at home, he betrays his sky wife for a terrestrial girl, and then, in the sky, he feels homesick again. Thus the whole sky episode ends on a negative position. In the second phase, when Asdiwal makes his first human marriage, a new set of oppositions are released: mountain-hunting and sea-hunting; land and sea.

Asdiwal wins the contest as a land-hunter, and in consequence is abandoned by his wife's brothers. Next time Asdiwal's marriage allies him with island-dwellers, and the same conflict between land and sea takes place, this time on the sea in a boat, which Asdiwal has to leave in the final stage of the hunt in order to climb onto the reef of rock. Taken together, these two phases can be broken down into a series of unsuccessful mediations between opposites arranged on an ever-diminishing scale: above and below, water and earth, maritime hunting and mountain-hunting. In the sea hunt the gap is almost closed between sea- and mountain-hunting, since Asdiwal succeeds where his brothers-in-law fail because he clambers onto the rock. The technique by which the oppositions are reduced is by paradox and reversal: the great mountain-hunter nearly dies on a little half-submerged rock; the great killer of bears is rescued by a little mouse; the slayer of animals now cures them; and, most paradoxical of all, the great provider of food himself has provender become – since he goes home in the stomach of a walrus. In the final dénouement, Asdiwal, once more a hunter in the mountains, is immobilized when he is neither up nor down, and is changed to stone, the most extreme possible expression of his earthly nature.

Some may have doubted that myths can have an elaborate symmetrical structure. If so, they should be convinced of their error.

Lévi-Strauss's analysis slowly and intricately reveals the internal structure of this myth. Although I have suggested that the symmetry has here and there been pushed too hard, the structure is indisputably there, in the material and not merely in the eye of the beholder. I am not sure who would have argued to the contrary, but myths must henceforth be conceded to have a structure as recognizable as that of a poem or a tune.

But Lévi-Strauss is not content with revealing structure for its own sake. Structural analysis has long been a respectable tool of literary criticism and Lévi-Strauss is not interested in a mere literary exercise.

He wants to use myth to demonstrate that structural analysis has sociological value. So instead of going on to analyse and compare formal myth structures, he asks what is the relation of myth to life. His answer in a word is 'dialectical'. Not only is the nature of reality dialectical, and the structure of myth dialectical, but the relation of the first to the second is dialectical too.

This could mean that there is a feedback between the worlds of mythical and social discourse – a statement in the myth sets off a response which modifies the social universe, which itself then touches off a new response in the realm of myth, and so on. Elsewhere, Lévi-Strauss (1962b, pp. 283-284) has shown that this complex interaction is indeed how he sees the relation between symbolic thought and social reality. And he even attempts to demonstrate with a single example how this inter-action takes place (1963b; cf. 1962b, Ch. IV). But in his analysis of myth itself he leaves out this meaning of dialectic. This is a pity, but perhaps inevitable because there is so little historical information about the tribes in question, and still less about the dating of different versions of the myth.

Rather, he develops the idea that myth expresses a social dialectic. It states the salient social contradictions, restates them in more and more .modified fashion, until in the final statement the contradictions are resolved, or so modified and masked as to be minimized. According to Lévi-Strauss, the real burden of the whole Ásdiwal myth and the one burning issue to which all the antinomies of sky and earth, land and sea, etc., are assimilated, is the contradiction implicit in patrilocal, matrilateral cross-cousin marriage. This comes as a surprise, since there has never been any mention whatever of matrilateral cross-cousin marriage in the myth of Asdiwal. But the Asdiwal story has a sequel. His son, Waux, grows up with his maternal kin, and his mother arranges for him to marry a cousin. He inherits his father's magic weapons and becomes, like him, a great hunter. One day he goes out hunting, having forgotten his magic spear which enables him to split rocks and open paths through the mountains. There is an earthquake. Waux sees his wife in the valley and shouts to her to make a sacrifice of fat to appease the supernatural powers. But his wife gets it wrong and thinks he is telling her to eat the fat, on which she proceeds to stuff herself until, gorged, she bursts and turns into a rock. Waux, now without either his father's spear or his wife's help, also turns into stone. With this story the Asdiwal cycle is completed. Waux's wife dies of glut, thus reversing the opening gambit in which Asdiwal's mother is started on her journey by a famine. So the movement set going by famine ends in the immobility of fullness. Asdiwal's marriages were all with strangers. Waux makes the approved Tsimshian marriage with his maternal cousin, but she ends by ruining him; the myth makes thus the comment that matrilateral cross-cousin marriage is nothing but a feeble palliative for the social ills it seeks to cure.

Lévi-Strauss points out that the Tsimshian, along with other Northwest Coast cultures, do not benefit from the equilibrium which cross-cousin marriage could produce for them in the form of a fixed hierarchy of wife-givers and wife-receivers. They have chosen instead to be free to revise their whole system of ranking at each marriage and potlatch. So they are committed to deep-seated disequilibrium. Following Rodney Needham (1962), one suspects that this far-fetched reference to Lévi-Strauss's theory of elementary structures of kinship is misplaced. There is no reason to suppose that matrilateral cross-cousin marriage among the Tsimshian is prescribed. However, in reaching these basic antagonisms of social structure, Lévi-Strauss feels he has got to the rock bottom of the myth's meaning.·

> 'All the paradoxes . . . geographic, economic, sociological, and even cosmological, are, when all is said and done, assimilated to that less obvious yet so real paradox which marriage with the matrilateral cousin attempts but fails to resolve . . . ' (*supra*, pp. 27, 28).

A great deal of this myth certainly centres on marriage,

though very little on the cross-cousin marriage which is preferred. Lévi-Strauss says that the whole myth's burden is a negative comment on social reality. By examining all the possibilities in marriage and showing every extreme position to be untenable, it has as its core message to reconcile the Tsimshian to their usual compromises by showing that any other solution they attempt is equally beset with difficulty. But as I have said, we cannot allow Lévi-Strauss to claim the real meaning of such a complex and rich myth. His analysis is far from exhaustive. Furthermore, there are other themes which are positive, not negative, as regards social reality.

In the first place, this area of Northwest Coast culture combines a very elaborate and strict division of labour between the sexes with a strong expression of male dominance. The myth could well be interpreted as playing on the paradox of male dominance and male dependence on female help. The first hero, Asdiwal, shows his independence of womankind by betraying his first wife. He is betrayed by his second wife, abandons his third wife, but in the sequel his son, Waux, dies because of his wife's stupidity and greed – so the general effect is that women are necessary but inferior beings, and men are superior. Surely this is a positive comment?

In the second place, the potlatch too is built on a paradox that the receiver of gifts is an enemy. One-up-manship, in potlatch terms, brings success, rank, and followers, but two-up-manship inflicts defeat on the opponent and creates hostility. Asdiwal went too far when he brought four huge bears down from the mountain to confront his empty-handed brothers-in-law. Here again, the myth is positive and true to life, so no wonder they abandoned him. The ambivalent attitude in Northwest Coast culture to the successful shaman is a third theme that can plausibly be detected in the myth. Great shamans are always victims of jealousy. Asdiwal, the great shaman, is abandoned. So the myth is plain and simply true to life.

I feel that we are being asked to suspend our critical faculties if we are to believe that this myth mirrors the reverse of reality. I shall return again to give a closer look at the social realities of Tsimshian life.

Mary Douglas

The ideas of reversal and of inversion figure prominently in
Lévi-Strauss's argument. First, he suggests that the myth is
the reverse of reality in the country of its origin. Then he has
formulated a curious law according to which a myth turns
upside down (in relation to its normal position) at a certain
distance from its place of origin. These are both developed in
the Asdiwal analysis. Third, a myth which appears to have no
counterpart in the ritual of the tribe in which it is told is found
to be an inversion of the rites of another tribe (cf. Lévi-Strauss,
1956). On this subject the stolid English suspicion of cleverness
begins to crystallize.

If ever one could suspect a scholar of trailing his coat with
his tongue in his cheek, one would suspect this law of myth-
inversion. The metaphor is borrowed from optics, without any
explanation of why the same process should be observed in the
unrelated science of mythics:

> 'When a mythical schema is transmitted from one population
> to another, and there exist differences of language, social
> organization or way of life which make the myth difficult to
> communicate, it begins to become impoverished or confused.
> But one can find a limiting situation in which, instead of being
> finally obliterated by losing all its outlines, the myth is in-
> verted and regains part of its precision' (*supra*, p. 42).

So we must expect that exported myths will give a negative
or upside-down picture of what the original myth portrayed.
Is the scholar being ingenuous, or disingenuous? He must
recognize that opposition is a pliable concept in the interpreter's
hands. The whole notion of dialectic rests on the assumption
that opposition can be unequivocally recognized. But this is an
unwarranted assumption, as appears from a critical reading of
his treatment of a Pawnee myth (Lévi-Strauss, 1956).

To demonstrate the relation of myth to rite he takes the
Pawnee myth of the pregnant boy. An ignorant young boy
suddenly finds he has magical powers of healing and the
makings of a great shaman. An old-established shaman, always
accompanied by his wife, tries to winkle his secret from him.
He fails, since there is no secret learning to transmit, and then
ensorcells the boy. As a result of the sorcery the boy becomes

pregnant, and goes in shame and confusion to die among wild beasts. But the beasts cure him and he returns with even greater power, and kills his enemy. The analysis distinguishes at least three sets of oppositions.

Shamanistic powers through initiation : without initiation
child : old man
confusion of sex : distinction of sex

Lévi-Strauss then invites us to consider what rite this Pawnee myth corresponds to. His problem, which seems very artificial, is that there is at first sight no correlated rite. The myth underlines the opposition of the generations, and yet the Pawnee do not oppose their generations: they do not base their cult associations on age-classes, and entry to their cult societies is not by ordeals or by fee; a teacher trains his pupil to succeed him on his death. But, as he puts it, all the elements of the myth fall into place confronted with the symmetrical and opposite ritual of the neighbouring Plains Indian tribes. Here the shamanistic societies are the inverse of those of the Pawnee, since entry is by payment and organization is by age. The sponsor and his sponsored candidate for entry are treated as if in a father-son relation, the candidate is accompanied by his wife, whom he offers for ritual intercourse to his sponsor. 'Here we find again all the oppositions which have been analysed on the plane of the myth, with inversion of all the values attributed to each couple.' The initiated and uninitiated are as father to son, instead of as enemies; the uninitiated knows less than the initiated, whereas in the myth he is the better shaman; in the ritual of the Plains Societies it is the youth who is accompanied by his wife, while in the myth it is the old man. 'The semantic values are the same but changed in relation to the symbols which sustain them. The Pawnee myth exposes a ritual system which is the inverse, not of that prevailing in this tribe, but of a system which does not apply here, and which belongs to related tribes whose ritual organization is the exact opposite.'

Mere difference is made to qualify as opposition. Some of the oppositions which Lévi-Strauss detects in myth are undeniably part of the artistic structure. But opposition can be imposed on any material by the interpreter. Here we have an unguarded example of the latter process. To me it seems highly implausible that we can affirm any opposition worthy of the name between cult organization with age-grading and entrance fees, and cult organization by apprenticeship without age-grading. Old male with wife versus young man without wife, and with confusion of sex, these seem equally contrived as oppositions. If the alleged oppositions are not above challenge, the whole demonstration of inversion falls to the ground.

Here we should turn to the relation of myth to literature in general. Lévi-Strauss recognizes that a myth is 'a work of art arousing deep aesthetic emotion' (Jakobson & Lévi-Strauss, 1962, p. 5). But he strenuously rejects the idea that myth is a kind of primitive poetry (Lévi-Strauss, 1963a, p. 210). 'Myth,' he says, 'should be placed in the gamut of linguistic expressions at the end opposite to that of poetry. . . . Poetry is a kind of speech which cannot be translated except at the cost of serious distortions; whereas the mythical value of the myth is preserved even through the worst translation.' He goes on in terms more emotional than scientific to declare that anyone can recognize the mythic quality of myth. Why does he want so vigorously to detach myth criticism from literary criticism? It is on the literary plane that we have his best contribution to the subject of mythology. He himself wrote a splendid vindication of his own technique of literary analysis by working it out with Jakobson on a sonnet of Baudelaire (Jakobson & Lévi-Strauss, 1962). This essay is an exercise in what T. S. Eliot calls 'the lemon-squeezer school of criticism, in which the critics take a poem to pieces, stanza by stanza, line by line, and extract, squeeze, tease, press every drop of meaning out of it' (Eliot, 1957, p. 112). After reading the analysis, we perceive the poem's unity, economy, and completeness, and its tremendous range of implication.

When the lemon-squeezer technique is applied to poetry it has a high rate of extraction and the meaning flows out in rich cupfuls. Furthermore, what is extracted is not a surprise – we can see that it was there all the time. Unfortunately, something goes wrong when the technique is applied to myth: the machine seems to spring a leak. Instead of more and richer depths of understanding, we get a surprise, a totally new theme, and often

62

a paltry one at that. All the majestic themes which we had previously thought the Oedipus myth was about – destiny, duty, and self-knowledge, have been strained off, and we are left with a worry about how the species began. When Edmund Leach applies the same technique to the Book of Genesis, the rich metaphysical themes of salvation and cosmic oneness are replaced by practical rules for the regulation of sex. When Lévi-Strauss has finished with the Tsimshian myth it is reduced to anxieties about problems of matrilateral cross-cousin marriage (which anyway only apply to the heirs of chiefs and headmen). It seems that whenever anthropologists apply structural analysis to myth they extract not only a different but a lesser meaning. The reasons for this reductionism are important. First, there is the computer analogy, for the sake of which Lévi-Strauss commits himself to treating the structural units of myth as if they were unambiguous. This takes us back to the basic difference between words and phonemes. The best words are ambiguous, and the more richly ambiguous the more suitable for the poet's or the myth-maker's job. Hence there is no end to the number of meanings which can be read into a good myth. When dealing with poetry, Lévi-Strauss gives full value to the rich ambiguity of the words. When dealing with myth he suggests that their meaning is clear cut, lending itself to being chopped into objectively recognizable, precisely defined units. It is partly in this process of semantic chopping that so much of the meaning of myth gets lost.

But there is another reason, more central to the whole programme. There are two possible objectives in analysing a piece of discourse.[2] One is to analyse the particular discourse itself, to analyse what has been said. The other is to analyse the language, seen as the instrument of what is said. No reason has so far been given to suppose that the structure of discourse is necessarily similar to that of language. But there is reason to point out that if the language analogy is adopted, research will look for a similar structure, a logic of correlations, oppositions, and differences (Ricoeur, 1963). We can say that the first kind of analysis, of what has been said in a discourse, aims at discovering a particular structure. This is what the literary critics do and what Jakobson and Lévi-Strauss did in 'Les

Chats', and what Lévi-Strauss in practice does most of the time. This kind of analysis is not intended to yield a compressed statement of the theme. It is not reductionist in any sense. The other kind of analysis discovers a formal or general structure which is not particular to any given stretch of language. For instance, the alexandrine or the sonnet form is not particular to a given poem, and to know that a particular poem has been written in sonnet form tells you nothing about what that poem is about. In the same way, a grammatical structure is formal. A book of grammar gives the conditions under which communication of a certain kind can take place. It does not give a communication.

Lévi-Strauss claims to be revealing the formal structures of myths. But he can never put aside his interest in what the myth discourse is about. He seems to think that if he had the formal structure it would look not so much like a grammar book as like a summary of the themes which analysing the particular structure of a myth cycle has produced. Hence the reductionist tendency is built in to his type of myth analysis. He falls into the trap of claiming to discover the real underlying meanings of myths because he never separates the particular artistic structure of a particular set of myths from their general or purely formal structure. Just as knowing that the rhyme structure is a, b, b, a, does not tell us anything about the content of a sonnet, so the formal structure of a myth would not help very much in interpreting it. Lévi-Strauss comes very near this when he says (Lévi-Strauss, 1957) that the structural analysis of a Pawnee myth consists of a dialectical balancing of the themes of life and death. It might have been better to have said that it was a balanced structure of pluses and minuses, or of positives and negatives. If he had actually used algebra to present the pattern he discerned, then Edmund Leach might have been less tempted to speculate on the similarity of mythic themes all over the world. He himself had found a structure of pluses and minuses in the Garden of Eden myth (1961) and remarked that the recurrence of these themes of death versus life, procreation versus vegetable reproduction, have the greatest psychological and sociological significance. But I think that their significance is that of verb/noun relations in language.

Their presence signifies the possibility of finding in them formal structures. But they are not the formal myth structures that we have been promised. These can hardly be knowable in ordinary language. If they are to be discovered special terms will have to be invented for recording them, comparable to the highly specialized terminology of grammar. To say simply that myth structures are built of oppositions and mediations is not to say what the structures are. It is simply to say that there are structures.

I will return later to the question of whether these formal myth structures are likely to be important for sociology. At this stage of publication (though three new volumes are in the press), Lévi-Strauss has not succeeded in revealing them. I should therefore do better to concentrate on the particular artistic structures he has revealed.

The meaning of a myth is partly the sense that the author intended it to convey, and the sense intended by each of its recounters. But every listener can find in it references to his own experience, so the myth can be enlightening, consoling, depressing, irrespective of the intentions of the tellers. Part of the anthropologist's task is to understand enough of the background of the myth to be able to construct its range of reference for its native hearers. To this Lévi-Strauss applies himself energetically, as for example when he finds that the myth of the creative Great Crow illuminates the themes of hunger and plenty in Tsimshian life.

From a study of any work of art we can infer to some extent the conditions under which it was made. The maidservant who said of St Peter, 'His speech betrays him as a Galilean' was inferring from his dialect; similarly the critic who used computer analysis to show that the same author did not write all the epistles attributed to St Paul. This kind of information is like that to be obtained from analysing the track of an animal or the finger-prints of a thief. The anthropologist studying tribal myths can do a job of criticism very like that of art critics who decide what 'attribution' to give to a painting or to figures in a painting. Lévi-Strauss, after minute analysis of the Asdiwal myth, could come forward and, like a good antiquarian, affirm that it is a real, genuine Tsimshian article. He can guarantee that it is an authentic piece of Northwest Coast mythology. His analysis of the structure of the myth can show that it draws fully on the premises of Tsimshian culture.

Inferences, of course, can also be made within the culture; the native listener can infer a moral, and indeed myths are one of the ways in which cultural values are transmitted. Structural analysis can reveal unsuspected depths of reference and inference meaning for any particular series of myths. In order to squeeze this significance out, the anthropologist must apply his prior knowledge of the culture to his analysis. He uses inference the other way round, from the known culture to the interpretation of the obscure myth. This is how he discerns the elements of structure. All would agree that this is a worthwhile task. But in order to analyse particular structures, he has to know his culture well first.

At this stage we should like to be able to judge how well Lévi-Strauss knows the social reality of the Tsimshian. Alas, very little is known about this tribe. He has to make do with very poor ethnographic materials. There are several minor doubts one can entertain about his interpretation of the facts, but the information here is altogether very thin. A critic of Lévi-Strauss (Ricoeur) has been struck by the fact that all his examples of mythic thought have been taken from the geographical areas of totemism and never from Semitic, pre-Hellenic, or Indo-European areas, whence our own culture arose. Lévi-Strauss would have it that his examples are typical of a certain kind of thought, a type in which the arrangement of items of culture is more important and more stable than the content. Ricoeur asks whether the totemic cultures are not so much typical as selected, extreme types? This is a very central question which every anthropologist has to face. Is *La Pensée sauvage* as revealed by myth and rite analysis typical, or peculiar, or is it an illusion produced by the method? Here we are bound to mention Lévi-Strauss's idea of mythic thinking as *bricolage*. The *bricoleur*, for whom we have no word, is a craftsman who works with material that has not been produced for the task he has in hand. I am tempted to see him as an Emmett engineer whose products always look alike whether they are bridges, stoves, or trains, because they are always composed of odd pieces of drainpipe and string, with the bells and chains and bits of Gothic railing arranged in a similar crazy way. In practice this would be a wrong illustration of *bricolage*. Lévi-Strauss himself is the real Emmett engineer because he changes his rules as he goes along. For mythic thought a card-player could be a better analogy, because Emmett can use his bits how he likes, whereas the *bricolage* type of culture is limited by pattern-restricting rules. Its units are like a pack of cards continually shuffled for the same game. The rules of the game would correspond to the general structure underlying the myths. If all that the myths and rites do is to arrange and rearrange the elements of the culture, then structural analysis would be exhaustive, and for that reason very important.

At the outset of any scientific enterprise, a worker must know the limitations of his method. Linguistics and any analysis modelled on linguistics can only be synchronic sciences. They analyse systems. In so far as they can be diachronic it is in analysing the before-and-after evolution of systems. Their techniques can be applied to any behaviour that is systematic. But if the behaviour is not very systematic, they will extract whatever amount of regularity there is, and leave a residue. Edmund Leach has shown that the techniques of Lévi-Strauss can be applied to early Greek myths, to Buddhist, and to Israelite myths. But I suppose he would never claim that the analysis is exhaustive. In the case of his analysis of Genesis, I have already mentioned above that the residue is the greater part.

Lévi-Strauss in his publications so far seems blithely unconscious that his instrument can produce only one kind of tune. More aware of the limitations of his analysis, he would have to restrict what he says about the attitude of mythic thought to time, past and future. Structural analysis cannot but reveal myths as timeless, as synchronic structures outside time. From this bias built into the method there are two consequences. First, we cannot deduce anything whatever from it about the attitudes to time prevailing in the cultures in question. Our method reduces all to synchrony. Everything which Lévi-Strauss writes in *La Pensée sauvage* about time in certain cultures or at a certain level of thinking, should be rephrased to apply only to the method he uses. Second, if

Mary Douglas

myths have got an irreversible order and if this is significant, this part of their meaning will escape the analysis. This, as Ricoeur points out, is why the culture of the Old Testament does not fit into the *bricolage* category.

We know a lot about the Israelites and about the Jews and Christians who tell and retell these stories.[3] We know little about the Australian aborigines and about the no longer surviving American Indian tribes. Would this be the anthropologist's frankest answer to Ricoeur? We cannot say whether the *bricolage* level of thought is an extreme type or what it is typical of, for lack of sufficient supporting data about the examples. But we must say that the *bricolage* effect is produced by the method of analysis. For a final judgement, then, we can only wait for a perfect experiment. For this, richly abundant mythical material should be analysed against a known background of equally rich ethnographic records. We can then see how exhaustive the structural analysis can be and also how relevant its formulas are to the understanding of the culture.

NOTES

1. See pp. 1-47 of this book. The next few pages constitute Dr Douglas's summary of Lévi-Strauss's text (see Introduction) [E.R.L.].
2. In what follows I am indebted to the Rev. Dr Cyril Barett, S.J. for criticism.
3. Lévi-Strauss's own justification for *not* applying his method to Biblical materials seems to rest on the proposition that we do not know enough about the ancient Israelites! (See *Esprit*, November 1963, p. 632) but cf. Leach (1966) *passim* [E.R.L.].

REFERENCES

ELIOT, T. S. 1957. *On Poetry and Poets*. London: Faber & Faber.
FORTES, M. 1959. *Oedipus and Job in West African Religion*. Cambridge: Cambridge University Press.
JAKOBSON, R. & LÉVI-STRAUSS, C. 1962. 'Les Chats' de Charles Baudelaire. *L'Homme* 2: 5-21.
LEACH, E. R. 1961. Lévi-Strauss in the Garden of Eden: An Examination of some Recent Developments in the Analysis of Myth. *Transactions of the New York Academy of Sciences*. Series 2: 386-396.
—— 1962. Genesis as Myth. *Discovery*, May: 30-35.
—— 1966. The Legitimacy of Solomon: Some Structural Aspects of

Old Testament History. *European Journal of Sociology* **7**: 58-101.

LÉVI-STRAUSS, C. 1955. The Structural Study of Myth. *Journal of American Folklore* **28**: 428-444. Reprinted with modifications in C. Lévi-Strauss, 1963a.

—— 1956. Structure et dialectique. In *For Roman Jakobson on the Occasion of his Sixtieth Birthday*. The Hague: Mouton. Reprinted in C. Lévi-Strauss, 1963a.

—— 1957. Le symbolisme cosmique dans la structure sociale et l'organisation cérémonielle des tribus américaines. *Serie Orientale Roma*, XIV. Institut pour l'Étude de l'Orient et de l'Extrême-Orient, Rome, pp. 47-56.

—— 1958. La Geste d'Asdiwal. *École Pratique des Hautes Études, Section des Sciences Religieuses*. Extr. Annuaire 1958-1959: 3-43. Reprinted in *Les Temps modernes*, March 1961 [see pp. 1-47 of this book].

—— 1958a. *Anthropologie structurale*. Paris: Plon. (English translation, 1963a. *Structural Anthropology*. New York: Basic Books.)

—— 1962b. *La Pensée sauvage*. Paris: Plon.

—— 1963b. The Bear and the Barber. *Journal of the Royal Anthropological Institute* **93**, Part I: 1-11.

NEEDHAM, R. 1962. *Structure and Sentiment*. Chicago: University of Chicago Press.

RICOEUR, P. 1963. Structure et hermeneutique. *Esprit*, November: 598-625.

WEIL, SIMONE. 1950. *Attente de Dieu*. Paris: La Colombe.

Nur Yalman

'The Raw : the Cooked :: Nature : Culture'

Observations on *Le Cru et le cuit*

'I was raw, I cooked, I burn . . .'

JALĀLU'D-DIN RŪMI

'. . . ce que vous cherchez . . . c'est un *sens des sens*, un sens qui est par derrière le sens; tandis que, dans ma perspective, le sens n'est jamais un phénomène premier: le sens est toujours reductible. Autrement dit, derrière tout sens il y a un non-sens. . . .'

CLAUDE LÉVI-STRAUSS: 'Réponses . . .'

(1963c, p. 637)

I

T. S. Eliot, in some of his most celebrated essays, developed the concept of the 'objective correlative'. It meant those features of the external world which, when referred to in poetry, could express sentiments which could not be conveyed by abstract words. Much of his own poetry exemplifies this insight.

Lévi-Strauss's attempt in *Le Cru et le cuit* is strictly parallel in its general intention. He tells us, in his first sentence, that the object of his book is to show how simple empirical categories, like raw and cooked, can be treated as conceptual tools to form abstract ideas which can then be interconnected in logical propositions. In other words, instead of the p and q of mathematical thinking, we shall have Jaguars and Wild Pigs related to each other in formal logic.

In the case of Eliot, the objects of the external world become the carriers or releasers of deep emotions; whereas Lévi-Strauss, on the contrary, underlines their function of carrying clear-cut ideas, particularly in myth and ritual. The similarities as well as the differences between the poet and the anthropologist are important. They indicate a fundamental agreement on the relation of the individual to his world through language, though one is on the emotive and the other on the cognitive plane.

The theme of how the elements of the external world are

71

used in the process of reasoning had already occupied the author in his general work on the structure of thought categories, *La Pensée sauvage* (1962b). To examine the matter in greater detail, it might be thought that his next step would have been to enter the well-equipped laboratories of experimental psychology and work on subjects from his own culture to facilitate the problems of communication.

Lévi-Strauss attacks the problem in *Le Cru et le cuit* from a diametrically opposed and strategically stronger position. Instead of the vagaries of the individual mind, he selects collective representations, and, instead of subjects from his own culture, he chooses some of the most exotic tribes of South America for a detailed analysis.

The greatest difficulty in this kind of work is that the data can be unmanageable. Just what kind of evidence is to be taken as exemplifying 'structure of thought categories'? Here Lévi-Strauss has decided to confine himself strictly to the data of mythology. Myths are clearly an example of the mental activity of people. They are furthermore 'collective representations' of a most important kind. His object, therefore, is to discover whether there is any logic behind the complex images and episodes described in the mythology of these tribes. If it can be shown that these myths have an underlying structure, then, argues Lévi-Strauss, it must be concluded that all levels of human activity must also be structured and determined. Again, the approach is that of structural linguistics. The myths are treated as communications in an unknown language which must somehow be deciphered.

In attempting to carry out this ambitious programme, which begins with the simple intention of analysing a single myth from the Bororo tribe, Lévi-Strauss conducts us through 187 myths from various tribes in South America. The collection of myths themselves would make a most fascinating document, but with Lévi-Strauss as a guide the volume becomes an aesthetic experience and a *tour de force* of analytical reasoning. It is safe to say, whether we consider Lévi-Strauss's endeavour to be successful or not, that it is unlikely for anthropologists ever to repeat the mistake of considering the content of myths to be unimportant or not worthy of attention *per se*.

In this volume, Lévi-Strauss succeeds in doing for the realm of myth what Radcliffe-Brown did for social structure. In other words, we take it for granted now that an isolated custom cannot be understood without the total structural context of which it is a part. Similarly, Lévi-Strauss demonstrates that a myth or its segments can be meaningfully analysed only in terms of the positions they occupy in the total myth structure of the culture concerned.

Lévi-Strauss likens this structure, which he progressively unfolds, to the structure of music. He had already suggested the similarity between music and mythology in his early essay on myth (1955, cf. 1963a, p. 212). It is an explicit position in this volume. So much so that the organization of the volume itself is in the form of a musical score.

To understand how an anthropologist and a specialist in the study of cross-cousin marriage has arrived at this remarkable position, we must examine the intellectual trajectory of this particular bombshell.

II

La Pensée sauvage, which marks an important point in the development of anthropological theory, has in fact been described by its author as being nothing more than a stage to catch his breath between two major efforts. The first is *Les Structures élémentaires de la parenté* (1949) and the second *Le Cru et le cuit* (1964). In the first work, the author attempted to undermine some of the basic assumptions of functionalist anthropology. In the exhaustive examination of marriage rules and practices, his intention had been to demonstrate the relative autonomy of the 'realm of rules' from economic, political, or other practical considerations. He tells us now that his attempt was not conclusive: for marriage rules, by their very nature, are interrelated with behaviour, and the analysis of their internal logical coherence cannot be divorced from their immediate consequences on a practical plane.

In attempting to demonstrate the autonomy of 'the realm of rules' from utilitarian matters, Lévi-Strauss is not concerned to show that mental activity is in some sense undetermined and free. On the contrary, his enterprise is intended to demonstrate that mental activity is completely determined down to its most insignificant manifestations. But, in his view, it is not simply determined by the facts of the 'infrastructure' – economics, politics, kinship, etc. – of which it has sometimes been assumed to be a mere epiphenomenon, but by 'mental constraints'. In other words, mental activity is determined by inner constraints of a categorical and logical nature, and there is a complex relationship between these and the facts of social existence.

In the present study of mythology the author finds justification for his enterprise in the fact that in myths the 'spirit' has nothing objective and practical to be concerned with: it is left to a *tête-à-tête* with itself, and it is precisely in these circumstances that the structure of cognitive categories can be demonstrated most effectively. Such are the underlying motives behind this exhaustive study of myths from one of the least known regions of the world.

III

In commencing his investigation, Lévi-Strauss places himself in as specific a context as possible: he provides full texts of myths collected from the Bororo tribe. The myths are then placed in their ethnographic context. They are concerned with, for instance, the making of penis sheaths for boys by women. We are provided with the detailed background to follow the analysis. Some episodes thus cannot be interpreted without a note on 'anus-stoppers'. But we soon find that the ethnographic commentary merely underlines even more sharply those aspects of the myth which cannot be further interpreted by this 'semantic' procedure. We are urged, therefore, to consider more carefully the internal 'structure' of the myths.

Lévi-Strauss does not enter into an extended discussion of his methodology in this volume. He is content to elucidate it by demonstration. There is little doubt that the reader, and particularly the specialists for the region, will find much to disagree about with the author. At times, Lévi-Strauss's movement from particular observations among the Bororo to very general observations regarding various oppositions of Nature/

Culture; High/Low; Sky/Earth is almost dizzying. But, in general, there is no doubt that he succeeds in demonstrating that the myths do not vary haphazardly, that there is a definite logical coherence to them, that elements which remain un-explained in one myth become clear in the analysis of other contrasting myths from the same or neighbouring tribes.

In his procedure the surface meaning is left aside, and the latent structure is elucidated by comparing the position of the elements of one myth with those of other similar myths.

It is here that the implications of the methods of structural linguistics become apparent. Just as the linguist is concerned with the syntactical structure of a message where he may analyse the structural position of the various elements, in the same way, by comparing myths in detail with each other, Lévi-Strauss indicates in what respects we may speak of similar or different structures.

It would not be possible in this paper to demonstrate how Lévi-Strauss derives the 'structure' of a myth from the detailed text. But the comparison of different versions of the same myth or similarly organized myths yields a strict symmetry of the kind indicated in the tabular diagram on p. 76.

It is not the case that the whole set of 187 myths can be compared as rigorously as in these three examples. Sometimes the reader feels left behind in the rapid movement of Lévi-Strauss's prose, at other times certain portions of the myths appear acceptably related, whereas other portions must wait until they can be analysed in the context of still other myths.

In this fashion, commencing with the incest and patricide of Geriguiguiatugo, the culture hero of the Bororo of Central Brazil, Lévi-Strauss moves on to the analysis of myths from the Ge, Sherente, Mundurucu, and numerous other tribes.

The exploration proceeds in great detail from myth to myth and, in the author's phrase, develops in the form of spirals, constantly harking back to motifs which have already been analysed. So, for instance, the author is able to show that the incest myth of Geriguiguiatugo is in fact related to the origin of cooking (i.e. the change from animal to human state) even though this motif does not appear manifested anywhere in the text of the myth itself. Thus there is a latent level to the myths

Mythical 'structures' (see *supra*, p. 75) [cf. Lévi-Strauss (1964, p. 141)]

M₅₅ 2 Animals	Ape > Rodent	Adventure on Water	Animal (<) too Audacious	Animal (<) exits (dead)
M₇ M₁₂ } 2 Men	Man A > Man B	Adventure on Land	Man (<) too Timorous	Man (<) exits (alive)
M₅₅ Animal (>) isolated	Meeting with Jaguar	*Negative Mediation – Ape-Jaguar* 1. Animal (water) (fish) offered and refused by Ape	2. Jaguar swallows Ape
M₇ M₁₂ } Man (<) isolated		*Positive Mediation–Jaguar-Man* 1. Animal (air) bird) demanded (and given by Jaguar	2. Jaguar does not swallow Man
M₅₅ Ape on top Jaguar below	Jaguar ogre	Conjunction imposed	Ape *in the stomach of* Jaguar
M₇ M₁₂ } Man on top Jaguar below	Jaguar food-provider	Conjunction negotiated	Man *on the back of* Jaguar

which can be grasped only by working through a large corpus of myths.

Lévi-Strauss then makes an immense détour through myths relating to the origin of pigs, of women, of tobacco, of the seasons and constellations, because certain aspects of the first myth continue to remain obscure even after determined efforts are made to clarify it as we move from one extraordinary myth to the next.

Thus, for instance, the reference in the first myth to the bad odour of lizards which Geriguiguiatugo has killed requires an examination of the general role of odour in all the myths. So we are given the 'Fugue of the Five Senses', a large section in which the role of all the senses and their symbolic implications are elucidated (Lévi-Strauss, 1964, pp. 44,155-171).

After many myths have been dissected, the author proposes some unifying concepts. He refers to Armature, Code, and Message. The Armature comprises those elements which remain constant in a number of myths; the Code is the interrelationship between the elements; the Message is the content of the elements. As one moves from one myth to the next, transformations take place in some of these respects.

The author notes in his delightful 'Overture', with which the work commences, that he is well aware of the ambiguities involved in the terms he uses such as symmetry, inversion, equivalence, homology, and isomorphism. These are not, in fact, the difficult concepts. What needs direct elucidation are the key concepts of 'transformation' and the logical grids of 'oppositions', on which the author pins his myths like peculiar but fascinating insects.

À propos of transformations, we are told that they permit the similarities of structure to be expressed in many different ways. The repetition itself, as in music, emphasizes the form that is behind the slight variations. Hence all the more reason to consider the cases of transformations in the myths carefully and in detail.

Regarding the 'oppositions', it is difficult to know whether they are merely heuristic devices to order the symbolism or whether they are categories of the native mind which evoke the myths by their interplay. But even with these reservations,

the precision of Lévi-Strauss's observations is always illuminating. For instance there is a long series of myths about Jaguars
in which the Jaguar saves the hero, teaches him the art of fire
and of cooking. Why does the Jaguar occur so frequently in
these myths?

Lévi-Strauss's comments take the following form:

Man and Jaguar are polar opposites. One eats raw food, the
other cooked food. Moreover Jaguar eats Man, but Man does
not eat Jaguars. There is no reciprocity between them.

But in the myths, all the 'cultural goods' Man possesses come
from the Jaguar. In other words, since mythical times, Jaguar
and Man have changed places. This suggests that there must
have been a reciprocity between them. And indeed it is true
that the Jaguar has a human wife. In many myths the Indian
wife of the Jaguar plays an important role in opposing the
culture hero. Once, however, the goods of the Jaguar have
been taken over by Man (usually his fire is stolen) then the
'connection' is broken and the human wife of the Jaguar is
destroyed. In a footnote on ethnography, the question is further
clarified. It appears that the Indians of Colombia, for instance,
regard the Jaguar not as any other animal but as an important
rival of Man. They both hunt the same animals. There are,
hence, ethnographic as well as internal logical reasons for
regarding them as being in opposition to each other.

One of the most telling demonstrations of transformations
occurs when we are shown how a Sherente myth M_{12}, regarding
the origin of fire, is related to the Bororo reference myth M_1,
which concerns the origins of tempests and rain (see Lévi-Strauss,
1964, pp. 43-45, 80-81, 145, 199).

In brief outline Myth$_{12}$ runs as follows:

One day, a man decides to take his young brother-in-law to the
forest to capture young parrots. The young man climbs a high
tree to get to the nest and, while his companion is waiting below,
takes a stone from his mouth and drops it down. On its way
down the stone changes into an egg which breaks. The companion is annoyed and deserts the boy at the top of the tree. A
Jaguar passes. He invites the boy to jump down, and catches
him. The boy is afraid but the Jaguar does not harm him.

The Jaguar then carries him away. The boy is thirsty and drinks up all the water without leaving a drop to the Crocodile.

The Jaguar's wife does not receive the boy well. But the Jaguar gives him a bow and arrows, ornaments, and roasted meat and sends him along to his village. The wife pursues him and is killed by the boy. Finally, the boy returns to the village on the occasion of a funeral rite.

Everyone is very astonished to see the roasted meat which he has brought with him. The secret of cooking is finally revealed to his uncle. An expedition, at which birds assist, is undertaken to steal the fire from the Jaguar.

The overt similarities between this and the reference myth M_1 are slight, but Lévi-Strauss points out that both are concerned with water and fire. In the Bororo myth, water (tempest) destroys all domestic fires. In the Sherente myth, the hero becomes the Master of the Water by taking the water away from the Crocodile who is the former Master of the Water. (It is the Crocodile's duty to prevent the Earth from drying up.) The hero later becomes Master of the Fire.

In both myths the heroes are bird-catchers and deceivers, and in both cases they deceive their own people in an unjustified and unnecessary manner.

In both myths, moreover, there is the motif of Death and Resurrection.

Beginning with similarities such as these, Lévi-Strauss shows that there is an inverse symmetry between the Bororo myth concerning the origin of rain and the Sherente myth concerning the origin of fire. This difference is linked up in a superb vignette with the ecological conditions in which the tribes live. The Bororo live in a watery element. Their way of life is partly on the ground and partly on water. In their religious beliefs, the water has an important role to play. Their dead have their flesh stripped from their bones and are then immersed in rivers or lakes, which are the habitat of souls. The Sherente are not particularly exposed to the risk of drought, but the fear of the sun drying up and consuming the earth is apparently very real to them.

So, the myths are to be understood in the context of all these ecological and religious factors. Water for the Bororo connotes death. And there is an association made between fire and life. With the Sherente, it is the other way around: they think in terms of droughts. Fire connotes death, and water is opposed to fire as a life-giving element.

It would be impossible and beyond our competence to enter into the detailed further implications of these ideas in the total conceptual schemes of the tribes with which Lévi-Strauss is concerned. The formal aspects of these demonstrations are, however, of more than immediate interest. For, on the basis of this demonstrated relationship between two myths from two tribes, our author moves on to an interesting exercise.

If we express the transformation relationship between M_1 and M_{12} as

$$M_1 \xrightarrow[(f)]{} M_{12} \qquad \text{or} \qquad M_{12} = fM_1$$

then in any general case where $M_y = f\, M_x$ we may expect to meet with a third myth M_z which has explored the opposite transformation, such that

$$\left[M_z \xrightarrow[(f)]{} M_x \right] \approx \left[M_x \xrightarrow[(f)]{} M_y \right]$$

(see Lévi-Strauss, 1964, p. 205).

In other words, then, is there a myth among the Sherente relating to the origin of water that is the inverse of the Bororo myth of the origin of water and that will demonstrate the above equations regarding the associations of Life and Death, Fire and Water, as well as the other episodes?

There is apparently such a myth (M_{124}), and its detailed analysis is certainly arresting. Suffice it to say that this myth not only commences with the initial incest of the Bororo case (that is, the Mother is violated by her elder sons) but goes on to invert specific elements of the initial Bororo myth point for point. Even such motifs as a passage which refers to lizards are repeated and altered.

In concluding this section, Lévi-Strauss notes that, since the Sherente see the Crocodile as Master of the Water and the Jaguar Master of Fire, it is logical that the origin of water confronts the hero with the Crocodile (M_{124}) just as the origin of fire confront him with Jaguars. Moreover, since water and fire are opposed, the behaviour of the animals and the heroes is inverted: the hero of M_{12} is courteous towards the Jaguar, whereas the hero of M_{124} treats the Crocodile insolently.

The light thrown upon even minute details of myths by Lévi-Strauss's close examination is quite surprising. They form part of a section entitled 'The Well-tempered Astronomy'. What is even more surprising, since it is hardly expected, is an amazing section in which, in order to show the association of the Constellation of Orion and Corvus, the Raven with the dry and the wet seasons in Brazil, the author takes an astronomical détour to examine the positions of these constellations in both the astronomy and the mythology of the ancient world. The Constellation of Orion is meteorologically linked up with the rainy season in the Athens of 1000 B.C. Is there a connection between twentieth-century Brazil and 1000 B.C. Athens? There apparently is, and what is more, it is faithfully (and inversely) reflected in the myths of Ancient Greece.

IV

Lévi-Strauss proves to be a reliable guide in this dangerous field. Many objections which soon enough begin to form in the mind of the reader are detected and raised by the author himself. It is only after he is on solid ground that the exploration once again gets under way.

The analysis remains faithful to the limits set to it by the author. That is to say, the myths are taken in their entirety. It is not merely the convenient or easily accessible parts that are analysed. No recourse is had to historical explanations or extraneous accidents: for, it is noted, if the analyst were to open the door to arbitrary explanations then all would be lost. How would one then choose between a logical explanation in one case and an arbitrary explanation in the next. In fairness to the author, it should be said that this difficult programme is faithfully carried out.

There are certain subjects on which doubt remains. Lévi-Strauss has argued that to understand a myth we must attend to the structure rather than to the tale (1963a, p. 214). But he had suggested a stricter structural analysis than is in fact carried out in this volume. In other words, in the present volume, he is not merely concerned with syntactic order in these texts but with semantic meaning as well. In one passage he notes directly that in the realm of myth form and content cannot be finally separated but that as one tries to separate them they return to interpenetrate each other. Hence, the justification – plausible and necessary – for providing quite condensed, but quite effective descriptions of the culture, concepts, philosophy, customs, and behaviour of these tribes. The only important cultural experience we appear to be denied are rituals. I should note that the interrelationship between myth and ritual is so complex and so important that we must assume that the almost complete silence on ritual must be taken to indicate a decision of the author to return to that siege with renewed forces in a different season.

Where do all these labours take Lévi-Strauss? The elucidation of one Bororo myth in fact leads him on an elaborate tour of the entire field of South American mythology. One myth refracts into the next, as one problem begins to take a manageable shape the next is already waiting resolution. At the end of the search, an immense distance is covered, but, though the basis is present, it does not permit a systematic presentation of a religious world-view. On the contrary, it is merely the impact of the orderly mind of the author which allows us to detect the latent principles of organization in this vast mass of extremely complex material.

But then is this symmetry in their minds, or in the mind of the observer? The question is barely touched on: what does it matter, says the author, whether their thought takes form under the impact of mine or mine takes form under the movement of theirs? This vulnerable position is acceptable so long as there is identity between the frameworks that are generated on their side and on the author's; but this identity is always suspect on technical grounds since, as Lévi-Strauss has observed in a famous essay, native models and the models of the anthropologists do not necessarily coincide.

The ultimate test of these peregrinations will be when specialists in the South American field have had their say, and when the new evidence has been assimilated and is brought to bear on Lévi-Strauss's extraordinary work. It should be noted, however, that the author's observations are based on an immense labour of scholarly groundwork. And specialists who disagree with him in this difficult terrain where there are no previously accepted ground-rules for methodical procedure, will not find it easy to dislodge the foundations of the fantastic edifice which has been constructed.

But architectural metaphors are inappropriate. As the author notes, the book is itself a myth and its construction is based on a musical metaphor. The basic themes are explored in the 'Overture': then they are stated in compact form in $Myth_1$, and the rest of the work keeps returning to these themes, they are picked up and taken along until other themes return. The point is made gracefully. Although other forms of presentation could have been chosen this one is effective.

How successful is the quest, then, into the 'inner constraints' of mental activity? Ricoeur, in criticism, has described Lévi-Strauss's position as 'un kantisme sans sujet transcendantal'. This formula Lévi-Strauss cheerfully accepts (1963c, p. 633). Since myths are 'collective representations' no particular 'mind' can be said to be responsible for them. In other words, the categories which may be discovered in the myths do not in fact correspond to those of any individual 'mind'.

But Lévi-Strauss is on solid ground. The fact that he has chosen very exotic tribes to demonstrate his point, heightens, the effect of the 'collective categories' which he ferrets out from the myths. At a certain level he is absolutely successful in demonstrating how their thought as evidenced in the myths does not reign free but is constantly channelled into particular patterns. Not only do we see the inner coherence of the patterns in any one of these cultures, but they make sense in contrast to the patterns around them. We are shown precisely how mythical thought is constrained by these receptacles into which it flows.

However, on the philosophical side an important objection remains: myths, like poetry, conform to standardized local conventions. They are not simply equivalent to 'thought'.

Nur Yalman

Is there a collection of dreams from the same tribes which would show the same patterns? Can these myths be seriously treated as an accurate reflection of the reasoning of these tribesmen?

The other problem that shows itself behind this one, and that exercises Lévi-Strauss, is whether it is possible to isolate some universal principles of thought from the staggering confrontation between their thought and his own? This is why he is so deeply interested in the difficulties encountered in this act of comprehension and translation of native categories into the terms of another culture. The problem is one of immense complexity. It is clear that certain areas of human experience are paralleled from culture to culture. From the theoretically unlimited impressions of earthly existence, some are selected for attention over and over again. Some of these, food, cooking, fire, water, the sun and the moon, light and darkness, high and low, male and female, generation and death, may be used as tools with which to build coherent systems of symbols. Lévi-Strauss moves into some of these controversial regions towards the last pages of the book. No naïve simplicity is to be expected here, but there certainly are audacious suggestions. For instance, the treatment of the eclipse in primitive societies and the custom of charivari are juxtaposed.

In the European tradition the charivari was undertaken upon the remarriage of widows, or when girls deserted a good suitor for one who was merely rich, aged, or a stranger, or when pregnant women married in white, or for young men who sold themselves to a woman for her money, and so on. In other words, the charivari was occasioned when there was an interruption in or reversal of the proper and expected order of events. The couple were met with a lot of noise. The eclipse, too, occasioned a great deal of noisy demonstration. Lévi-Strauss notes that with all the noise they are trying to chase away, in one case, an astronomical monster which is devouring the sun and, in the other, a 'sociological' monster who is altering the proper order of things.

From these beginnings, the author moves on to an investigation of the role of noise/silence in the myths and customs of many cultures. He shows how noise is often associated with reprehensible unions (though many negative examples of noise

84

at wedding ceremonies in the Near East and Ceylon immediately
come to mind), whereas proper unions demand silence. Thus
the domestic fire (a symbol of great importance), which unites
the earth and the sun, demands silence, in contradistinction to
eclipses, which are met with noise.

It cannot be said that these ideas on universal thought
categories are taken very far. But in these days when most
anthropologists tend to take total relativity of cultures and
complete permutability of human experience for granted, it is
worthwhile to observe some efforts to synthesize the position
and to attempt at least to detect basic experiences which may
be repeated even in very exotic cultures (Leach, 1958).

Lévi-Strauss makes humble claims. He says that he hopes
to have left the field in a less bad state than it was before.
Those who disagree with him should, indeed, take a look at
some myths from South America which have not been analysed.
One can see them in their raw state, for instance, in Fock (1963).
The motifs of climbing trees and jaguars all reappear again but
remain as obscure as the myths collected from other parts of
the world.

The immediate effect of this work will be to place serious
burdens on the fieldworker. The kind of detailed micro-analysis
which Lévi-Strauss has undertaken demands a fairly large set
of myths from the societies concerned. Few anthropologists,
one suspects, who have concentrated their work on social
structure or even on religion would also be able to produce
voluminous evidence on mythology in the native language. The
question is of considerable importance for it bears both upon
new directions in fieldwork and on the method of analysis of
religious material. For the lesson of myths is equally applicable
to ritual. The analysis must proceed not on general impressions
and the opinions of the informants on various subjects
haphazardly collected but on a systematic analysis of a body
of very detailed material, such as a collection of myths or an
entire series of rituals.

One of the most important criticisms to be levelled against this
work is formalism. Lévi-Strauss applies his own method
vigorously: he is single minded in attempting to trace connec-

tions of a formal nature between the myths in this collection. But what does this analysis show about the thinking processes of the tribes in question? What indeed is the relationship between the relatively formal myths and the rest of the mental activity of the tribes? Can the myths be taken as an accurate reflection of their thought even in religious matters? And, finally, what is the relationship of the many formal patterns indicated by the analyst to the expressed customary attitudes of the people? Are some conscious and the others unconscious? We are not told where the natives' thought and explanations end and those of the author begin.

On the formal methodological level where the myths are merely regarded as messages to be deciphered, the distinction between conscious and unconscious symbols is obviously redundant. But as soon as we move away from this formal posture and ask about interconnections with other aspects of the culture, especially with ritual, then we must know the logical status of the author's interpretations: are they only heuristic models and only to be applied to myth, or is the symbolism conscious and a part of accepted custom?

On the theoretical level, Lévi-Strauss's method of myth analysis bears some admitted resemblance to the dream analysis of modern psycho-analysis (Lévi-Strauss, 1963b, p. 648). Yet the position of the author regarding the other methods of symbol analysis of Freud or the collective unconscious of Jung – which are implicitly rejected – is not clarified. Hence the problem of the unconscious remains open.

These are serious questions which can be resolved only by abandoning the full rigour of Lévi-Strauss's method. As long as one is totally immersed in myths as evidence, one is trapped in a play of mirrors in which one moves from reflection to reflection. Here one must get away from the images and steal a glance at the angles of the walls on which the mirrors are mounted.

The achievement of having shown that there are formal patterns in the realm of myth is not to be underestimated. But the relationship between this part of the 'superstructure' and other aspects of the mental activity remains obscure. Unless the role of these formal categories in the rest of the mental and ritual life of the tribes can be shown, the charge of formalism will be difficult to evade.

Some of these nagging questions may be settled when the dynamic connection between the realm of the 'superstructure' (myth) and the realm of the 'infrastructure' (social organization, economy, etc.) is analysed by the author. We may surmise that this must be the next step in his progression. At this point ritual plays a vital role. It is probably the one important point of contact between the realms: for no doubt some of the myth episodes are expressed in ritual, and no doubt again the total pattern of ritual is related to the social structure of the tribes. Since this path of investigation, which could have provided an important link with the ethnography of the region, is not explored in this work the reader is left in something of a quandary regarding the status of the vast symbolic system which is unfolded before him. How do the various tribes handle their corners of the system? Lévi-Strauss might reply that, by using the same logical categories, the various tribes have simply evolved different transformations, but what is the status of these systems in connection with the total ritual life of any one of these peoples?

As one moves with Lévi-Strauss from tribe to tribe and myth to myth, the emphasis is on the 'transformations' from one pattern to the next. The author contends that this procedure is legitimate since all the groups are culturally and historically related. But this only raises a further problem. Is the entire constellation logically related or are there historical survivals from earlier periods involved? If it is both, then, can the entire system be subsumed under one previous super-system which originally contained all the 'transformations' in latent form? This brings us back again to the problem of mathematical logic.

Leach (1964), in a fascinating paper, had underlined the relation between the symbolism of primitive peoples and mathematical symbolism and had suggested that there was indeed something in common in the mental processes involved. Lévi-Strauss, in the book under discussion, amply demonstrates this thesis that there is mathematical logic behind the very complex manifestations of mythical symbolism. In other words, the sense of order and symmetry which is constantly to be observed in all manifestations of culture, is a reflection of certain features of our mental apparatus shared by *homo sapiens*. So myths, at least in one respect, are a primitive form of mathematical thinking.

Finally, we should observe that this approach, if it has any value, should be meaningfully applicable to the particularly important field of religious myths which usually enjoy a privileged freedom from such rational onslaughts in their secure gardens. All the world religions rest on sacred foundations of myth. In their richness, the Jewish, Christian, Muslim, Hindu, and Buddhist mythologies (and their 'transformations') present a luxuriant field for the mythological anthropologist that would certainly keep him busy for a long time.

As a result of Lévi-Strauss's strenuous efforts, it is only fair to admit that we have arrived at a watershed in social anthropology. With this formidable work, the long-held view that forms of social organization are the main if not the only area of inquiry worthy of serious attention by anthropologists is taken off its pedestal. Lévi-Strauss, following the clues left by many thinkers before him, has found his way into an immense area of human experience which remains uncharted, full of traps and all kinds of theoretical monsters. It will never be possible again to treat the mental life – myth, ritual – of the people we have been concerned with as a mere epiphenomenon of the 'concrete' facts of economics, politics, and kinship.

Since we have tended to regard myth and ritual as something of a hodge-podge of symbolism, as weird psychological quirks emanating from the obscure darkness of the unconscious, it was easy to behave as conquistadors and merely grab what came to hand and overlook the most fascinating aspects of culture. It was also easy to imagine that the field had to be abandoned to psycho-analysts, who had better tools to handle the problems raised by such work. This extraordinary volume makes it clear that there is much serious thinking to be done on this subject by anthropologists, and that the practical and methodological difficulties will tax our resources to their utmost.

The study of the structure and functions of customary

thought still lies in the future. On this terrain, though Lévi-Strauss is certainly not the first adventurer, he may turn out to be the first successful cartographer.

REFERENCES

FOCK, N. 1963. *Waiwai: Religion and Society of an Amazonian Tribe.* Copenhagen: National Museum of Denmark, Ethnographic Series, Vol. 8.

LEACH, E. R. 1958. Magical Hair. *Journal of the Royal Anthropological Institute* **88**, Part II: 147-164.

—— 1964. Telstar et les aborigènes: ou 'La Pensée sauvage'. *Annales* No. 6, Nov.-Dec. Paris.

LÉVI-STRAUSS, C. 1949. *Les Structures élémentaires de la parenté.* Paris: Presses Universitaires de France.

—— 1955. The Structural Study of Myth. *Journal of American Folklore* **28**, 428-442. Reprinted with modifications in C. Lévi-Strauss, 1963a, pp. 206-231.

—— 1958a. *Anthropologie structurale.* Paris: Plon (English translation, 1963a. *Structural Anthropology.* New York: Basic Books).

—— 1962b. *La Pensée sauvage.* Paris: Plon.

—— 1963c. Réponses à quelques questions. *Esprit*, No. 322, Nov.

—— 1964. *Mythologiques: Le Cru et le cuit.* Paris: Plon.

K. O. L. Burridge

Lévi-Strauss and Myth

I

The subject of myth is, and has been, anybody's plaything. And because Claude Lévi-Strauss is 'one of the few', a truly great anthropologist who is at once fecund and seminal, as original as he is ingenious, the subject, Lévi-Strauss himself, and Lévi-Strauss's mode of dealing with myth must first be given some general placement.

Most students of culture would agree that their central concern is an understanding of developmental processes. And for anthropologists in particular the central problem remains tied to a still unresolved opposition between History on the one hand and Evolution on the other. Whether the question is how and by what means some hominid crossed 'the threshold' to become *Homo sapiens*, or the movement from one kind of economic or political or symbolic system to another, the same dilemma emerges: how, given a positivist approach and so debarred from a useful if often treacherous transcendentalism, may one reconcile the implications of History with those of Evolution? Given an Aristotelian respect for the so-called 'facts' of ethnography, how, other than by admitting a Platonic primacy for thought and idea, may such 'facts' be given an appropriate relevance?

Ever since the diffusionist criticism made the dilemma apparent, anthropologists have sought to escape from or reconcile the implications of man as a plaything of nature and evolutionary forces, on the one hand, and man as the arbiter of his fate, stamping the environment with his thought, on the other. Ever since the establishing of the fieldwork tradition – roughly coinciding with the diffusionist criticism – anthropologists have been aware that the inescapable moral relationship between observer and observed precludes anything but a highly coloured and multivalent relevance to an observation. Unable

91

to measure accurately everything they observe, unable to repeat and so re-examine a situation, often disinclined to note what may be repugnant to themselves as moral observers, anthropologists have been forced to seek their common departures or 'objectivity' within the schemes or 'languages' of their more illustrious predecessors. And these 'languages' coincide with those devices – such as description and analysis modelled on the natural sciences or 'Marxism' or 'functionalism', or 'structure' or 'topology' or 'statistics', 'numeration', 'communications systems', and the like – which seek either to evade or to approach a reconciliation of the primary terms of the dilemma.

Within such a context the study of myth or myths is of crucial importance. Myths are reservoirs of articulate thought on the level of the collective. But they are not simply 'articulate thought' in a vacuum. They represent the thought of people about themselves and their condition. Moreover, the words of a myth, especially when set down in writing, appear to have an 'objective' existence irrespective of the attitudes and approaches of narrator, listeners, or observer. The question is whether Lévi-Strauss has provided us with a 'language' capable of resolving the dilemma as between History and Evolution, capable of dealing with myth as a social representation as opposed to dealing with myth as a linguistic phenomenon simply.

II

Three features of the work of Claude Lévi-Strauss seem to be relevant here. First, that he is interested in thought, in logic, in modes of articulate thought. Again and again he comes round to saying in one way or another, 'The same logical processes are put to work . . . man has always been thinking equally well . . . the improvement in thinking lies not in any alleged progress in man's conscience, but in the discovery of new things to which it may apply its unchangeable abilities' (1963a, p. 230). Second, in his address to this problem of articulate thought, Lévi-Strauss appears to lean heavily on Hegel who, it will be remembered, sought to reconcile the events contained in the progress of history with God and human mental activities or mind; and this largely through the formula 'thesis – antithesis – synthesis', the method of the dialectic. Third, while eschewing Hegel's transcendentalism, Lévi-Strauss's handling of ethnographic materials seems coloured by a Darwinian evolutionism on the one hand and Marxian thought on the other.

Regarding 'Hegel', 'Marx', and 'Darwin' as shorthand characterizations, and recognizing in them the ingredients of the very dilemma which we have already identified, we may say, very briefly and in summary terms, that for Hegel truth or reality consisted in the unification of contradictory elements: and these elements, representing partial aspects of truth, were to be related not only as contradictory but also as logical contraries. An idea or object which seemed to the mind to possess a unity could be broken down into contrary and contradictory elements, and these elements could themselves be further broken down into successive contraries and contradictions. In attempting a synthesis, the building-up of a unitary idea or object from a variety of elements, the same process was involved. This, the method of the dialectic, represented for Hegel a 'negative' reason: it was sceptical, dislocating, even temporarily destructive. Where 'thesis' stood for unity or a unitary formulation, 'antithesis' stood for a breaking-down of this unity into contraries which were also contradictions, and 'synthesis' stood for a rebuilding of the unitary.

In Hegelian terms experience exists within the limits of the categories of language. And even if Hegel had had the benefit of the formulations of Freud or Jung, one cannot see him allowing validity to an experience that could not be reduced to language, the vehicle of the collective. Not simply a question of linguistics, of grammar, phonemes and syntax, the categories of language – the categories of articulate thought – formed, for Hegel, a system with their own laws and relations which appeared in a less obvious form in the theories of nature and the mind. That is, the workings of the mind and the vehicle through which it expresses itself determine not only the ways in which we interpret the workings of nature and ourselves, but the ways in which we view the workings of the mind itself – a theoretically infinite interplay between the mind and its object which is exemplified in the use of, and the thought about, computing machines and communications engineering as well as in the way Lévi-Strauss handles totemism (1962a) – and, indeed, most topics apart from kinship (1949).

Assuming, as one must, a general familiarity with Lévi-Strauss's work, the summary passages above may show something of his reliance upon Hegel. The encounter with Marx is no less interesting. Marx, one might say, seized upon the 'contradictory' rather than the 'contrary' in Hegelian thought, and on the 'material' rather than the 'idealistic' elements in Hegel's dialectic. If, for Hegel, the dialectical process was logical, ontological, and chronological, the dynamic of history lying in the 'Idea', divinely inspired, Marx seems to have taken from Hegel process, progress, the method of the dialectic, the impersonality of history, and the priority of the collective. But he rejected the metaphysical, the theological, and, to a certain extent, the ethical content of Hegel's system. Eschewing, too, the Hegelian gloss of the 'hero' as an embodiment of the collective will, Marx seems to have thought of the 'collective' as necessarily implying a 'group' or 'class', and certainly concentrated upon that dialectical process which is defined and expressed by the struggle for power as between different economic classes or groups within a given environment. But in spite of this narrower and more satisfying definition of the problem in contrast to the much wider and larger Hegelian view, the dilemma is not simply one between a 'larger' and 'narrower' view. Rather does it reside in a logic and an ontology which assume the existence of God, on the one hand, and an empiricism and a materialism which negate the existence of a transcendent deity, on the other. Or, to put it more sharply, 'In the beginning was the word', the primacy of articulate thought as definitive of man, and from which culture flows, as against an economic determinism which, if initially based upon cultural features, has become muddled with environmental determinism and ideas borrowed from biology and evolutionary theory.

Between these two standpoints, there can be no real compromise. If the first acknowledges and admits the force of the second, realizing through the use of the active voice that there must also be a passive, the second can hardly accommodate the first – even though, in fact, the habitual use of the passive tends to invest the active 'natural' or 'evolutionary', or 'social' forces with some vague but always convenient transcendentalism. And though most anthropologists, as it seems to me, tend to try to avoid the implications of these contrary positions by the use of private eclecticisms, by the use of active or passive as occasion seems to demand, in doing so they fall into a trap which seems also to have claimed Lévi-Strauss. For, while Lévi-Strauss accepts the primacy and priority of thought, in his handling of ethnographic data he feels constrained to take a materialist standpoint. Unable to accept a transcendental ontology in relation to the problem of thought, he assumes an evolutionist position by taking 'nature' as his widest context of relevance. His 'nature', indeed, corresponds on the whole to Hegel's 'God'. Never clear about the difference between a 'contrary' and a 'contradiction', to whom particular features appear as either one or the other, whether what appears as logically 'contrary' is necessarily ontologically 'contradictory', when a 'contrary' is not a complementarity, or in what circumstances a 'contradiction' is not a complementary opposition, Lévi-Strauss seems to me to be continually attempting to reconcile and resolve three very recalcitrant terms: Hegel, Marx, and that eclecticism which, while reluctant to admit the real animality of man and so the implications of that animality, still insists upon using the more pleasing and flattering aspects of biological evolution while seeking to pin the cultures of man to particular environmental bases.

We may carry these points a little further. In the last chapter of *La Pensée sauvage*, where he engages with Sartre on whether or not 'analysis' is compatible with 'dialectic', Lévi-Strauss clearly favours Hegel as against Marx. For, apart from following Hegel in arguing that 'analysis' is contained in, and indeed is, the dialectic, he goes on to say that logical contraries in themselves contain a dynamism of process. Which is a restatement of Hegel – providing that the contraries are also contradictions. Then again, in the last few sentences of *Tristes Tropiques*, there is a quite remarkable reference to exchanging a wink 'with a cat' (1955a, p. 449; 1961, p. 398). And it is not an aside, it is a final fling. What on earth does he mean, if he means anything? What kind of communicative experience is he trying to instance? If one thinks for a moment of the refractions of meaning involved in *La Pensée sauvage*, the interminable dialogue between the mind and its object is inevitably evoked and the whimsical reference to the cat looks like either the shy admission of an ontology based on a mutual participation in 'nature', or, since cats are notoriously disdainful, the admission that the cat cannot relevantly exist outside perceptions of what it might be.

Still, if only because life is relatively short, there must come a point at which the dialogue between the mind and its object may be taken to be concluded. And, it seems to me, Lévi-Strauss finds this terminal within the positivist and materialist limits set by Marx coupled, however, with a regard for 'man in nature'. That is, where Marx is concerned with 'man in society', Lévi-Strauss would seem to want to transcend the empirical facts of observation in a particular view of 'nature': which is an escape from Marx into Hegel, even if it is a Hegel on Lévi-Strauss's own terms.

In a discourse based upon the empirical observation of different cultures a pertinent question, in moving towards the general statement, is at what point and with reference to what kind of vocabulary may a generalization subsume the mass of empirical observations. Lévi-Strauss's answer is in some contrast to most of those to be found in the history of the development of anthropology in Britain and the United States – though the dilemma is the same. On the one hand, there are resorts to eclectic pragmatisms and biological, introspective, technological, and statistical models, a marked reluctance to become 'either history or nothing', a determination to pursue a comfortable middle way, while, on the other hand, there is the realization that the new knowledge[2] may not be as new as all that, and that the central opposition of History and Evolution is best evaded by tapping the springs of thought of the great systematists. Lévi-Strauss was a pupil of Mauss. And if all the members of that community of scholars which one thinks of as the 'French School' owe much to each other, for Lévi-Strauss the debt is greatest to Hegel and Marx rather than to Durkheim or Comte or Montesquieu.

All this is simply to emphasize that if Lévi-Strauss succeeds

96

Lévi-Strauss and Myth

in representing himself to some of us as alternately windy, or deft, or overgiven to confusing metaphors or ironies, or stimulating, or as clever as the boatswain of yore, it is not only because he belongs to a not wholly familiar tradition, but because he is absolutely his contrary self. Not a Marxist, through Marx the bare bones of an ethnographic record are given coherence. Not wholly a Hegelian, at the level of total social fact, and in relation to articulate thought, a Hegelian treatment is demanded. Not a Darwinian, man in nature is his base.

III

Though Lévi-Strauss's main concern is with the subject of articulate thought, is with the relations between 'the word', 'being', and 'process', myths – which might have pushed him further along the path of his main problem – become for him, on the whole, simply data by means of which an attempted resolution of the Hegelian and Marxian dialectics may be demonstrated. In attempting to reconcile the positive and the transcendental, however, Lévi-Strauss is himself contrary. If he criticizes what he calls the 'functionalist position', making it clear that he thinks that myths ought to be understood as 'things in themselves' without reference to the culture which produced them, his own 'La Geste d'Asdiwal', when compared with his analysis of the Oedipus story in 'The Structural Study of Myth', shows how much more satisfying his method can be when it is related to the culture concerned. Again, the rather laboured passages in 'The Structural Study of Myth' in which he opposes *langue* to *parole*, *traduttore*, and *tradittore*, and goes on to say that the language of myth is the opposite of poetic because it does not suffer from translation (1963a, p. 210), are contradicted by his own acute use of the meanings of words in both 'La Geste d'Asdiwal' and 'Four Winnebago Myths' (1960a). And vagary comes into full flower with the suggestion that American foundations might well lay aside thousands of dollars for the structural analysis of myth!

Behind the whimsy and irony, however, as often hidden in as revealed by the clutter of analogies and asides, an obviously powerful and exciting mind is at work. So, quite briefly, Lévi-Strauss's basic approach may be summarized as follows:

97

1. The whole of culture may be regarded as a communications system. Myth is but a particular form of communication.

Just as one may use the dialectic to analyse culture as a whole, so with myth. To find out what a myth is communicating, the elements must be broken down into pairs of contraries and their resolutions. This breakdown is the structure. What are these elements? Stemming from the dilemma as between Marx and Hegel, Lévi-Strauss is verbose but nothing if not ambiguous. On the whole, however, since myths are to be understood as things in themselves, and though his previous best work would deny just this, by 'elements' he means translated words.

2. Lévi-Strauss does not oppose sociology to psychology: instead he contraposes psychology and structure.

This is an important point. In the first place, since the word 'sociology' hardly appears in Lévi-Strauss's work it seems futile to assume that he means by 'structure' any one arbitrarily chosen reference of the many attached to 'sociology', or that his 'structure' coincides with any one particular usage in English. In the second place, since psychology – *pace* those social anthropologists who still like to think that psychology is concerned only with the single individual and weaning – attempts to systematize human relationships and interrelationships, the distinction which Lévi-Strauss is making seems to be one between form and content, category and behaviour. What interests Lévi-Strauss is not so much what people do, or why they might do what they do, but what they should be called when they do it. Form and category are determined by language rather than by other kinds of behaviour.

3. Lévi-Strauss refuses to be pinned down by the implications of the differences between 'contrary' and 'contradiction'.

This is consistent with his overt refusal to consider content, as well as with the model he draws from structural linguistics.

Is this model taken from structural linguistics a sufficient or complete picture of what Lévi-Strauss means by the 'structure of a myth'? One may speak of the structure of a short story being contained in the formula *situation – complication – resolution – rider or twist*, where the last term provides a new situation itself capable of being complicated if necessary, resolved, and followed by a further rider. And at this level the formula could be said to represent the 'structure' of all or most short stories. By applying the formula to successively smaller parts of the whole story one would eventually have the 'structure' of a particular short story. Moreover, if the formula corresponds to the dialectic cycle, since it refers at any level to contradiction and conflict in terms of content, it is Marxian rather than Hegelian – in the sense that Marx would neglect contraries of verbal form, emphasizing contradictions of situational content or organizational incompatibilities, whereas Hegel would not admit such a contradiction unless he could find it to imply a logical contrary and *vice versa*. As I understand him in what he does as opposed to what he says one ought to do, Lévi-Strauss's notion of 'structure' in relation to myth is an attempt to marry the kind of formulation instanced above with that part of the Hegelian system which refers to logical contraries.

Consistently applied this, I think, would be good. But Lévi-Strauss is not consistent. Where Hegel insisted that 'contrary' and 'contradiction' – the statement about the behaviour and the behaviour itself – should coincide or correspond to each other, and Marx emphasized the element of 'contradiction', leaving the 'contraries' or statements about the behaviour to look after themselves, Lévi-Strauss employs an *ad hoc* and arbitrary mixture of both systems, overtly inclining to emphasize the 'contrary' only. Given this mixture of dialectics, and given the common experience of the fieldworker writing up his data that apparent contradictions on one level appear as harmonies or consistencies on another, the methodology itself will predicate what a particular myth 'is about'; and what a myth 'is about' is likely to be arbitrary in one sense or another. Lévi-Strauss wants it both ways, and he attempts to reconcile the opposed positions of Hegel and Marx in the formula, '. . . the purpose of myth is to provide a logical model capable of overcoming a (real) contradiction' (1963a, p. 229). That is, a myth informs its bearers of contradictions in life, and then it

attempts – as I would prefer to put it here – to explain them
away.

Is this really what myths do or 'are about'? Let us be clear.
If Lévi-Strauss often gives the impression that he is almost
contemptuous of the futilities of men, he is always concerned
with the uniqueness and primacy of Man – particularly with his
definitive attribute, articulate thought. Really what a myth
'is about' or is 'telling' us or its bearers is, for Lévi-Strauss, a
secondary consideration, a by-product of the main point at
issue: the structure of articulate thought. Further, what
Lévi-Strauss wants to demonstrate – as against, for example,
such writers as Lévy-Bruhl – is the universality of the processes
of articulate thought. Symbols, things, and particular relations
may differ from culture to culture, but the address of the
human mind towards them is the same – 'unchangeable'.
Moreover, it is just this 'sameness' that constitutes the
'structure'. Whether the context involves one or more cultures,
'structure' is to be found at that level of abstraction which
resolves apparently different relations into corresponding
relations or 'sameness'. In his approach to myth, that is,
Lévi-Strauss attempts to demonstrate the assumption that used
to be known as the 'psychic unity of mankind'; and his notion
of 'structure' is predicated by the point – which must vary
according to context – at which differences are merged in
sameness or correspondence. Which is excellent if correspondences refer to relations or sets of relations in their content, not
so happy perhaps where form and category are not necessarily
derived from content.

Having made these points about Lévi-Strauss's usage of the
term 'structure', his opposition to 'psychological explanations' –
though he never makes it clear except by implication what
kinds of explanation these are or can be – as well as his
reluctance to talk about 'sociology' or 'sociological' become
clearer. By 'psychological explanation', Lévi-Strauss cannot
mean simply explanations which lean on, or are borrowed from,
psychology or psychologists. These are part and parcel of our
general ambience of ideas. He means, presumably, that kind of
explanation in which the investigator assumes that the cultural
experiences and reactions of the people under survey are, or

are almost, identical with his own at their own levels – or that kind of explanation which depends upon a shifting and ethno-centric concept of 'normality' and is not referred to an objective and persistent formal collective. And for Lévi-Strauss this objective collective is to be discovered in language, in the categories of articulate thought. If it can be shown that all peoples everywhere think articulately in the same way, have the same logic, then this logic will provide the common frame-work within terms of which any culture may be described and analysed. Hence, perhaps, the reluctance to use the term 'sociology'; 'sociologies' tend to come in different and not wholly compatible varieties.

'Structure', for Lévi-Strauss, is concerned with logical categories and the form of the relations between them. He explicitly eschews, though in fact in this he is as guilty as most of us, those verbose circumlocutions which so often conceal explanations referable not to a collective form but rather to an author's private emotional state or psychology, or are at bottom a 'herd instinct' or 'natural proclivity' kind of explanation. Further, such interest as Lévi-Strauss has in social relations, in the ways in which offices, groups, statuses, roles, and the rest are related, is simply a preliminary towards elucidating 'total social fact' – normally linguistically and adjectivally deter-mined – and then the logical structure which appears to contain these relations.

Lévi-Strauss's priorities may, therefore, be summed up as follows:

1. Structure, in which are entailed—
    (a) the primacy of the collective,
    (b) extrication from involvement in concrete behaviour,
    (c) a frame of reference which has objective value, if it can be shown that the processes of thought follow a universal logic.
2. The 'structure' of thought.
3. The use of myth to demonstrate (1) and (2) above.
4. Almost incidentally, as it were, to elucidate what the myth 'is about' in terms of content and communicative meaning.

Given these priorities, and coming closer to the specific problems, the purpose of myth, says Lévi-Strauss, is to provide a logical model capable of overcoming a real contradiction. Elements of the myth (thesis) are to be broken down into pairs of contraries (antithesis), resolved through mediators (synthesis and thesis), and further broken down into contraries (antithesis again) which are to be resolved again in mediators (synthesis and thesis) only to be broken down yet again into contraries.[3] These elements – which I have suggested tend in fact to be words – tend to be restricted in number in any particular myth, and are themselves composed of further elements whose different combinations – of the kind b-a-t, r-a-t, t-a-r, t-a-b – provide the inner contradictions and mediations which, in turn point to the main contradiction which it is felt that the myth is trying to 'explain away', or provide a logical model capable of overcoming or reconciling.

IV

How does all this work out?

Both critique and appreciation are provided by examining a very short myth collected in New Guinea:

Once upon a time the leading man of the village was fishing by the light of his bamboo torch in Cipenderp stream when it came on to rain. The leading man and all the other men and women of the village took shelter under the lee of a large stone. The last to come were a boy and his sister, orphans. They were dirty, unwashed, and smelly.

'Hey! You two can't come in here!' exclaimed the leading man. 'You smell too much!'

The storm increased in intensity, the rain poured down, the two orphans sought shelter in a hollow tree.

Seeing what had happened, the Great One on High sympathized with the orphans. He caused the stone to envelope the villagers.

The orphans returned to the village, mourning their fellows. Later they tried to crack open the stone. It was no use. They killed all the pigs in the village, collected piles of foodstuffs and, with the help of neighbours, put all the meat and tubers by the stone.

It was no good. The villagers died of hunger inside the stone.

Some preliminary points. I cannot honestly say that I wholly follow Lévi-Strauss's treatment of the Oedipus story in 'The Structural Study of Myth'. In what follows I am not attempting to be, or be like, Lévi-Strauss. I am simply going to try to follow his instructions. If I end up by demonstrating an inability to follow him, well, perhaps a critique is implied. Further, since we have been asked to deal with Lévi-Strauss in relation to our own fieldwork, it becomes virtually impossible to detach oneself from a host of 'prejudices' as to what the myth is 'really about'. And, finally, if the purpose of myth is to overcome a real contradiction, and one has particular kinds of contradiction in mind, then it will no doubt be possible to find these contradictions. There are few purposes a myth will not adequately serve.

Putting the story onto cards, then (1963a, p. 211), resulted in not just one pack but three slightly different packs. So, by slipping round some facets of meaning which I thought I knew were there, I reduced the three packs to one. Four results are worth setting out, the first on Lévi-Strauss's Zuñi model, the others on the Oedipus model.

The initial situation may be broken down into the 'contraries' 'light' and 'darkness', which may be said to be mediated by 'stream'. For, since a stream flows on in the same way whether it is light or dark, it is unaffected by the contraries and so resolves them. But a stream is water, water is rain, and rain is the source of the stream: we get the contraries 'in the rain' and 'out of the rain'. This pair is resolved in the notion of 'shelter' which is itself broken down into 'good' people in one kind of shelter and 'smelly' – or, as is the case if we take note of the cultural content of the vernacular terms – 'bad' people, the orphans, in another kind of shelter: stone, which makes cultural tools, as opposed to hollow tree, a wild or non-cultural place. If these contraries are mediated by more rain, the latter introduces the Great One who, in two contexts, further separates

103

the orphans from the 'good' people. We are left with the shadowy presence of the Great One, and the orphans who, one may presume, restart community life through an incestuous union. As between 'good' people and 'bad' people, or the Great One and community, or the Great One and the orphans, or incest and non-incest, or perhaps dual origin and single origin (orphans, Great One), which is the main contradiction that the myth is attempting to overcome by the positing of a logical model?

Turn now to the Oedipus example. A first result may be obtained by picking out relationships which are characterized by aid or reciprocity and opposing them to relationships in which non-reciprocity appears as definitive. Thus the leading man and the villagers, the Great One sympathizing with the orphans, and the orphans putting food against the stone may be opposed to the villagers and leading man excluding the orphans, the Great One enveloping the villagers, the Great One not acceding to the wishes of the orphans. What is left to go into the other two columns? 'Rain' and 'shelter', 'in the rain' as opposed to 'out of the rain'. Perhaps we may resolve this in the formulae, *Reciprocity : Shelter :: Non-reciprocity : Rain*; or *Reciprocity : Non-reciprocity :: Shelter : Rain*; or, by a rearrangement of the terms above, and ignoring things or phenomena, *Brother-and-sister incest : Reciprocity :: Self-will of the Great One : Good people in community*.

So far as I am concerned, knowing the culture, all the formulae obtained are good. But, again, I leave it to the reader to assess whether they are the kind of formulae Lévi-Strauss would like, and to state the real contradiction that is being overcome.

Take another result. Forget reciprocities and substitute relations of 'exclusion' and 'inclusion'. This yields the following: *Inclusion : Incest :: Bamboo torch and shelter : Exclusion*; or, *Inclusion : Exclusion :: Bamboo torch and shelter : Rain and hollow tree*; or, *Exclusion : Community :: Brother-and-sister incest : Inclusion*; or, *Hollow tree : Shelter :: Incest : Community*; or, *Exclusion : Inclusion :: Incest : Community*. One could in fact go on. The last is probably the best from Lévi-Strauss's point of view because it does not bring in concrete things. Still, I have brought in these concrete things in order to go back to them presently. Let us say, though, that by combining all the

results so far obtained, the 'real contradiction' between
reciprocity and non-reciprocity, or between inclusion in
community and exclusion from community, is logically resolved
or explained away by the notion that incest is non-human or
non-social. And then let us impose upon the myth Lévi-Strauss's
favourite contraries Life and Death, which he also seems to
assume imply a contradiction.

Here pause for a moment. . . . For in his usage of Life and
Death Lévi-Strauss seems persistently to assume the standpoint
not only of an individual but of a very particular individual –
what life and death may mean to him, how these contraries
may be resolved on the level of the myth for an individual. Is
this not precisely that worst kind of psychologism against
which Lévi-Strauss so inveighs? For most peoples death is but
a passage from one kind of being to another, and as a passage
death usually corresponds to birth and the movement from
child to adult – the kind of movement in which Hegel would
have delighted. But if Life and Death are to be taken as
relevant 'contraries' and 'contradictions' then they should be
referred to the collective, to the culture or community concerned: the survival or death of the community. And if we do
take Life and Death in this way, and not as Lévi-Strauss
would appear to regard them, we arrive at the formula,
Life : Death :: Community : Incest (between brother and sister).
Which is good. Yet we could go even further. For, granting that
death is but a passage from one kind of being to another, the
same formula could be used in the case where a traditional
community is dying and a new one is emerging. Which is
precisely the burden of the Hegelian dialectic, but not what
Lévi-Strauss seems to have in mind.

However, given the results above, what, in particular, is the
myth 'about'?

The first point that emerges is that if the method works the
answer is predicated by the initial address. Given the dialectics,
and given that the purpose of myth is to provide a logical model
capable of overcoming a real contradiction, if it is not clear – at
least to me – in what sense real contradictions are overcome,
it is demonstrable that contraries appear to be resolved, and
that the structure of thought might be the same as elsewhere.

K. O. L. Burridge

But, and it needs to be repeated, the results seem to spring from the imposition of a particular mode of thought rather than from the material. Someone who was resolved to show that the structure of articulate thought as demonstrated by the myth was different might be able to do so. And the riposte would be, I suppose, that since differences have been elicited the investigator has not been working at the level of structure.

The second point that emerges is that, given Lévi-Strauss's technique, or 'language', or mode of address, much more might be done.

v

To see how much more might be done, and for the purposes of a more constructive critique, turn now to an approach that climbs blatantly upon Lévi-Strauss's broad back and goes to content rather than the form. Given that culture is the primary and prior reality to be examined, allow primacy of place to articulate thought which may express itself in words, in a carving, or in other ways. Instead of attempting to peg the parts of culture to contingent facets of nature, physical environment, biology, instincts, or proclivities, let us be content with clusters of mutually defining relations – to start with at any rate. Suppose that a myth is a mode of cognition, not simply communication, which informs its bearers of the possibilities of awareness in the culture concerned. Suppose we say that the resonances of words do matter, and that in this sense mythical language, *contra* Lévi-Strauss, is poetic. Suppose we use an old literary technique and, quite coincidentally, try to demonstrate Lévi-Strauss's own dictum in relation to totemism . . . not 'good to eat, but . . . good to think' with (1964a, p. 89). Then further suppose that, for heuristic purposes, we separate myth (Myth) from the rest of culture (Culture) and attempt a dialogue between the relevant parts contained in the two main terms – what do we get?

It is neither practicable nor, indeed, necessary to proceed to a full and exhaustive demonstration of what is involved in the approach summarized above. It is sufficient to show the potential. Take first, 'bamboo torch'. In the culture, bamboo is used in a variety of ways as a container, primarily for water and for cooking strips of pig-meat. More dramatically, however, bamboo slivers were used as razors for circumcising boys, and the circumcisor was a mother-brother.[4] In the corpus of myths available in the culture, bamboo frequently occurs in association with mother-brother and circumcision, but only rarely explicitly as a razor. Yet within the dialogue Myth-Culture – and it should be remembered that the myth is not there on a piece of paper, but is being presented to an audience each of whom knows the myth, knows what has happened and what is going to happen next – we may speak of bamboo as evoking circumcision, the meaning of circumcision, and particular relevances of the mother-brother. Indeed, if one goes through the whole corpus of the mythology to which the story of the orphans belongs, substituting 'circumcision' for 'bamboo', the correspondences turn out to be very precise. That is, in Myth the word 'bamboo' means, signals or stands for, or evokes 'circumcision'. Since, however, the contextual references of 'bamboo' in Myth vary in certain particulars, and these latter provide additional resonances of meaning, we can in the end obtain reasonably accurate and objective indications of the thought about the relations between father, mother, son, mother-brother, and circumcision. Further, these indications of themselves cannot but throw 'water', 'pig-meat', and 'light' into a more meaningful perspective. All of which is at the least very useful when, as happens to be the case, circumcision is no longer practised.

Second, consider the word 'shelter'. Both in Myth and in Culture a 'shelter' is primarily shelter from the storm; and the word 'shelter' in fact connotes community and culture as distinct from the forest and natural world, the controlled and ordered as distinct from the uncontrolled or uncontrollable and unordered or wild. After a close scrutiny of the mythology, and after a process of testing and retesting, we find that 'roof thatch' is a synonym for 'shelter', and that both terms stand for, indicate, or evoke a clubhouse and associated organization, now defunct, known as the *garamb*.

The *garamb* was a men's house. Boys spent a period of apprenticeship there, and the climax to this was circumcision, a rite which took place in or near the *garamb*, and which is said to have 'made a boy into a man'. Indeed, circumcision qualified a youth for marriage, set him on the road to full manhood, gave him full membership of the clubhouse where responsible men foregathered. So that the word 'shelter' in its varying contexts both in Myth and in Culture indicates something of the thought about the relations between the clubhouse and the rite of circumcision.

Yet we may go even further. Men, but not boys, it is represented in the Culture, were originally made from the flesh of a pig; and when a youth was circumcised father had to provide him with a 'pig of the circumcision'. So that it is not just 'men in the beginning' who were made from pig-flesh, but all men as they become men and are circumcised. 'Light', we would come to know, is associated with whiteness, with an appropriate passage of the *garamb* through circumcision, with responsibility in the moral community, with the ability to see and so be aware of what is entailed in moral responsibility. 'Darkness', on the other hand, is associated with the wild, with the colour black, with blindness, and so with the inability to see and be aware, with sorcerers who, excluded from the moral community, paint their faces black when engaged in their nefarious and amoral activities. In the corpus of myths water is always the stuff from which the seminal male element emerges; maidens who are about to become wives go down to the stream to fish, rain is associated with semen, and the storm – thunder, lightning, and earthquake (which latter is represented in the stone enveloping the villagers) – generally figure male attributes, particularly those qualities which a father ought to pass on to his son, and which are thought of as having been passed to the son when, upon the son being circumcised in or near the *garamb*, father presented the pig of the circumcision. . . .

Certainly, the myth may be said to be providing a 'logical model' capable of overcoming the 'real contradiction' between reciprocity and non-reciprocity, or between inclusion in community and exclusion from community. And certainly, paraphrasing Lévi-Strauss and his Oedipus model, one could say that the myth provided a logical model capable of overcoming the 'contradiction' between the decisive and singular seminal power of the male (the Great One), on the one hand,

and the necessity to maintain the incest taboo and marry a woman who is not a sister, on the other. Certainly, too, most of the formulae we have obtained from a use of Lévi-Strauss's method are good, informative, so far as they go. But do they go far enough? Somehow one wishes that the formulae obtained by Lévi-Strauss's method could have told us that the myth not only was about incest but also indicated what was involved – or what was involved in thinking about – the qualities of maleness, fatherhood, the particular features of the father-son,[4] the role of the *garamb* and the mother-brother, the value of circumcision, how a youth grows into responsible manhood, the nature of moral responsibility, and why dirty and smelly people should not have access to the *garamb*. . . .

For the purposes of the rather slight demonstration above, we have but taken two words, words referring to things, 'bamboo torch' and 'shelter'. Even so, the beginnings of a symbolic system, of clusters of interrelated features, have become evident. Yet a complete examination would involve extending the scrutiny to include the referents of the categories of characters and relationships as well as of things in themselves. Thus the evocations of stream, rain, bamboo torch, shelter, stone, hollow tree, pig, and foodstuffs may be related to leading man, orphans, Great One, neighbours, and further related to leading man and community, orphans and leading man and community, Great One and orphans, Great One and community, orphans and neighbours, brother and sister. . . . Only after one has examined a myth on its own terms within the context of a corpus of myths, and discovered the idiom of myth, does it become possible to enter into a meaningful dialogue between Culture and Myth.

One result of the engagement between the two forms of collective is, of course, an incomparably richer understanding of the culture concerned. And for most anthropologists this ought to be reward enough. Another result is that one can obtain at least an outline of the symbolic system within which the members of a culture have their being, and this in terms of interrelated clusters of ideas which are themselves quite clearly tied to, or more closely associated with, particular sets of activities. Further, since the engagement is on the level of the collective, since two forms of collective are being engaged as thesis-antithesis to yield a synthesis, one may obtain a reasonably precise evaluation of the possibilities of awareness which a particular culture holds out to its members, and different kinds of awareness may be seen as attaching to particular processes in the life cycle as well as to particular relationships. Finally, since in any culture people relate their myths to each other, and discuss them, so subtly changing their content, whether one is examining 'Coronation Street', sacred stories, or the story of the two orphans, the encounter between living people and their myths precisely corresponds to the dialogue between Myth and Culture, and is, indeed, the living dialectic of history.

VI

Claude Lévi-Strauss's pioneering contribution to the study of myth will take its place beside Rivers's 'Genealogical Method' as one of those essential techniques upon which anthropological studies depend. Even so, it seems to be a limited technique, a technique which is self-explanatory and self-justifying. Which is why it has been found necessary to offer an alternative approach: internally, on his own ground, Lévi-Strauss's method is unassailable simply because it is self-justifying and self-explanatory. And so far as the suggested alternative approach seems to promise more than Lévi-Strauss's mode of address, thus far may one be justified in feeling that the alternative is more useful. Given that the alternative has not been, and within the scope of this paper cannot be, fully demonstrated, and given that its promise must be in the nature of assertions which cannot possibly be fulfilled entirely, still there seem to be good reasons, beyond mere usefulness, for choosing to use it rather than follow Lévi-Strauss. So, assuming for the moment that we are not dealing with a mere personal difference of concern or interest, with a division of labour within a particular field, it is worth while concluding by summing up what is involved in the two approaches.

1. Either the term 'culture' connotes a field of study which exists within its own right, something *sui generis* which flows from and expresses and articulates thought, to be examined on

its own terms as a complex of interior and mutually defining relations whatever the kinds of abstraction that may be made from it; or culture must ever be subject to those exterior anchorages which are, most usually, reductionisms of a biological or physical environmental kind.

The approach suggested here plumps for the first alternative: culture is irreducible, depends upon words and articulate thought, and should be studied in terms of itself. Maybe there is a relation between culture and environmental conditions, just as there may be a relation between madness and phases of the moon. But medical science would scarcely have advanced as far as it has if it insisted on anchoring all illnesses to the movements and phases of heavenly bodies. Lévi-Strauss is unclear and ambiguous on the matter. He seems to want Hegel and Marx and Darwin where he can only have Hegel or Marx or Darwin.

2. Lévi-Strauss's whole argument in 'The Structural Study of Myth' rests on the direct translatability of myth, on the assumption that the language of myth is non-poetic, that a myth may be translated without any concern for the resonances of words on either hand. If I have not actually demonstrated that the meanings and resonances of words can be decisive, then Lévi-Strauss's own 'La Geste d'Asdiwal' does. Not only is Lévi-Strauss, in fact if not in explicit statement, ambiguous about biological and environmental reductionisms, but he wants to anchor the terms of one culture in the terms of another. The alternative approach suggested rests on giving the resonances of words their full values. Only in this way, it seems to me, may we arrive at correspondences in relations rather than correspondences dependent on adventitious translations. Witchcraft among the Azande does not correspond to witchcraft in England; but there are sets of relations in England which do correspond to witchcraft relations among the Azande. The exotic vocabulary of anthropology has been a screen, not a door – as Lévi-Strauss himself has illustrated in relation to totemism.

3. Though he is nothing if not consistently ambiguous, on the whole Lévi-Strauss goes to form rather than content. The approach suggested emphasizes content, regarding form as

111

simply a convenient if revealing mode of ordering the content in a particular cultural context.

4. Lévi-Strauss ignores Hegel's insistence that a contrary should also be a contradiction, and he leaves out of account whether what is contrary, or a contradiction, in one culture is necessarily so in another. To be sure, there is no reason why he should stick to Hegel if he does not wish to do so. Nor is he under any compulsion to be rigorously Marxian. But in explicitly expounding a methodology dependent on the meanings of 'contrary' and 'contradiction' there is a need for precision. 'Life' and 'Death' are certainly 'contraries'. But in what sense are they necessarily 'contradictions'? By 'contradictions' we normally refer, surely, to goal-directed activities, or on-going processes, which effectively and simultaneously negate each other. 'Life' and 'Death' are alternatives: either 'alive' or 'dead'. A 'real contradiction' would involve, at any level, the experience of 'life' and the experience of 'death' at one and the same time. Which is unusual without shading in the meanings of 'life' and 'death'.

5. Despite his formal strictures against 'psychologisms', Lévi-Strauss frequently falls into just this trap. In his use of 'life' and 'death', for example, those favourite contraries of his, Lévi-Strauss evidently has in mind the meaning of 'life' and 'death' for himself or for an imaginary individual. The alternative approach suggested would, on the other hand, relate such a contrary to the collective. Thus incestuous relations of themselves do not necessarily predicate the deaths of particular people; but they would, for example, predicate the death of a culture built on exchange relationships dependent on the incest categories.

6. The history of anthropology is studded with formulations as to the purpose of myth. If we must keep to Lévi-Strauss's terms – that the purpose of myth is to provide a logical model capable of overcoming a contradiction – then, since all myths in fact present an audience with quasi-concrete situations, it is just as adequate to say that myths provide concrete situations capable of overcoming logical contradictions. Which is to reveal Lévi-Strauss's assertion as of the kind which asks whether the purpose of the skull is to keep the ears apart, or whether the

ears are separated in order to allow for the skull. Myths serve many purposes, almost any purpose. The problem, surely, is not to discover a particular purpose but, since myths are a part of total culture, to systematize their value as modes of cognition, as parts of that on-going process which Hegel thought of as the dialectic of history, and which the engagement between Culture and Myths seems to offer.

7. Finally, an initial hesitation in offering an alternative procedure as critique rather than making piecemeal criticisms of Lévi-Strauss on his own ground has been overcome by several considerations. One can only criticize or evaluate in the light of alternatives. Lévi-Strauss is extremely persuasive. Like the children who followed the pied piper, once caught by the jigging beat of binary oppositions, enthusiasts may jump for joy, not caring whether the next meal is raw or cooked. Like Freud, Marx, or Jung, Lévi-Strauss offers us a sweet-scented haven with many floral bowers in which to dally – or so it might seem. Yet perhaps it is an Erehwon. For Lévi-Strauss's method seems to impose a spurious uniformity on the material, spurious because order springs not from the encounter between investigator and data but from the categories of a closed system which cannot admit further possibilities. It negates the whole task of discovering the different kinds of forms within which the same sets of relations are organized or given coherence. All myths become much the same, dealing with the same things in the same ways. Yet it is evident – at least to the present writer – that this is just what myths do not do. Methodologically, Lévi-Strauss's procedure seems to represent much the same kind of imposture as was made by those of our predecessors who, by defining religion, law, economics, and political system in particular ways, could conclude that such and such had no law or religion, or political system, or economics. What of the singular and unbifurcated? Obsessed as he is with binary oppositions, with pairs and contraries, Lévi-Strauss seems scarcely to notice that contemplation and accommodation of the idea of the singular which could be said to lie at the roots of civilized life.

In conclusion, lest it be thought that these last paragraphs undervalue Lévi-Strauss, let it be stressed that the formulae

K. O. L. Burridge

obtained by Lévi-Strauss's method in relation to the story of the two orphans are all good. I know they are good, and, having access both to the culture and its mythology, more than anyone else I can appreciate how good they are. The issues are whether the empirical exercise, fieldwork, can invalidate Lévi-Strauss's method – I do not see how it can – and whether such formulae as may be produced are self-explanatory or refer to something other than themselves. If fieldwork cannot invalidate a method – should the method be followed? If formulae are self-explanatory – can they pose any further problems?

NOTES

1. All references in this paper are to works by Lévi-Strauss listed below.
2. Sir John Myres quotes Tylor as saying that in the early days of Anthropology in Oxford 'Theology, teaching the True God, objected to false gods; Literae Humaniores knew only the cultures of Greece and Rome; Natural Sciences were afraid that the new learning would empty their lecture rooms'. *Proceedings of the five-hundredth meeting of the Oxford University Anthropological Society*, February 1963, p. 7.
3. 'The function of the repetition is to make the structure of the myth apparent . . . a myth exhibits a "slated" structure which comes to the surface . . . through the process of repetition. However, the slates are not identical. And since the purpose of myth is to provide a logical model capable of overcoming a contradiction (an impossible achievement if, as it happens, the contradiction is real), a theoretically infinite number of slates will be generated, each one slightly different from the others. Thus, myth grows spiral-wise until the intellectual impulse which has produced it is exhausted' (1963a, p. 229).
4. The expressions 'mother-brother', 'father-son', refer to a category of relationship rather than to a particular individual, cf. a series of the author's papers on Tangu in *Oceania*, Vols. 24, 27, 28, 29, 30.

REFERENCES

LÉVI-STRAUSS, C. 1949. *Les Structures élémentaires de la parenté.* Paris: Presses Universitaires de France.
—— 1955a. *Tristes Tropiques* (English translation, 1961. *A World on the Wane.* London: Hutchinson).
—— 1958. La Geste d'Asdiwal. *École Pratique des Hautes Études, Section des Sciences Religieuses.* Extr. Annuaire 1958-1959: 3-43. Reprinted in *Les Temps modernes*, March 1961.
—— 1960a. Four Winnebago Myths: A Structural Sketch. In S. Diamond (ed.), *Culture in History: Essays in Honor of Paul Radin.* New York: Columbia University Press.

—— 1962a. *Le Totémisme aujourd'hui* (English translation, 1964a. *Totemism*. London: Merlin Press).

—— 1962b. *La Pensée sauvage*. Paris: Plon.

—— 1963a. *Structural Anthropology*. New York: Basic Books. (All references to this work in the present paper are to Chapter XI 'The Structural Study of Myth' first published in 1955.)

PART II

The Structural Study of Totemism

E. Michael Mendelson

The 'Uninvited Guest'

Ancilla to Lévi-Strauss on Totemism and Primitive Thought

Discussing totemism, for Lévi-Strauss, is a matter of classifying classifications. First, we have the way in which a given social group divides the universe into classes, frequently containing both a human sub-group and some kind of animal or plant between which an association is postulated. Second, we have the way in which anthropologists classify the classifications made by different social groups. Third, we have the way in which these two activities themselves invite comparison in the context of the philosophy of science. Lévi-Strauss's 'Uninvited Guest' is the human mind and much of both the difficulty and the fascination of his work arises from the fact that this guest is both judge and plaintiff in a new anthropology. First, structural linguistics and psychology, later communication theory generally, provide the framework of the discourse and we cannot move towards it satisfactorily without acquiring its rudimentary vocabulary.

Taking the Professor in Telecommunication in the University of London as our guide, we find that the exciting Parnassus invoked by Lévi-Strauss is peopled by a number of not-so-young dames, including linguistics and psychology, clustered around the firm-fleshed young pin-up called statistical communication theory (Cherry, 1957). The older dames, referred to at one point as the 'method-starved ones', are warned that the mathematically rigorous scanties worn by their queen will not fit them without considerable adjustments, though it is hard to restrain their enthusiasm for the desirable new fashions.

A communication event, in its simplest form, supposes that something passes from a second something to a third something. Statistical communication theory concerns itself with *how much* of the first something gets through from the second to the third when the resistance of the medium it passes through, the

119

surrounding distortion, the power of expression of the second something and power of comprehension of the third are all taken into account. This is all mathematically rigorous and concerns anthropology very little in that such 'how much' questions are relatively far from our basically qualitative concerns.

Examined in these terms, linguistics reveals itself as a branch of semiotic, the theory of signs, a sign being defined as 'a transmission, or construct, by which one organism affects the behaviour or state of another, in a communication situation' (Cherry, 1957, p. 306). Three levels of study for signs are set in decreasing order of abstraction from real life: syntactics (signs and their interrelations), semantics (relations between signs and their designata), and pragmatics (signs in relation to their users). Linguistics, then, deals with communication events between emitters, senders, or speakers and receivers or listeners. The structure of the language communicated offers the speaker a particular choice of patterns which he selects to fit his intention. The patterns are picked up by the listener from his own knowledge of the structure. For practical purposes we can replace 'structure of the language' here by the word 'code', defined as 'an agreed transformation, or set of unambiguous rules, whereby messages are converted from one representation to another' (Cherry, 1957, p. 303, see also p. 7). To prevent confusion, another distinction is necessary at this point. In communication theory, a language is an organically developed primary instrument of communication which need not necessarily 'talk' logically: indeed, most humans are not notorious for cold logic. One refers to a language under observation as an 'object-language'. In order to talk *about* language, however, the scientist needs a rigorous, logical language, which, for the sake of convenience, is baptized a 'metalanguage'. Clearly, the term 'code' has relevance only in the context of metalanguage: we do not, for instance, converse with friends entirely in 'yeses' or 'nos'. With his theory of models and 'transformation systems', it is quite clear that Lévi-Strauss intends to create for anthropology a metalanguage: empirical observation as such remains below the metalinguistic level and does not accede to science. For this reason all our classifying of classifications to date, our whole theory of totemism, is, as it were, pre-scientific.

The point about the code being known to sender and receiver should be clear: your most frantic messages in morse would not reach me if I did not know morse. Mention of morse will remind you that the elements of this code are basically two: short dashes and long dashes form the alphabet. In a similar fashion, Jakobson (the linguist who has had the greatest influence on Lévi-Strauss) shows that the basic constituents of a human language – phonemes, can be shown to pair off into groups of two according to articulatory distinctive features: they are either vocalic/non-vocalic, voiced/unvoiced, grave/ acute, etc., up to twelve sets.[1] We are here in the presence of the famous 'binary opposition' principle upon which centres a great deal of communication theory. It is with binary codes (whose recognition is older than we sometimes suspect) that complex messages are fed into computers, bounced off Telstar, transmitted within the brain or along the genetic chain from parent to offspring. Binary opposition is the basis of Boolean algebra and thus, through Russell and Moore, of modern logic and mathematical thinking. We are obviously dealing here with something of great importance.

We are aware that life is an endless process of making choices between alternatives and hardly need a psychologist to tell us that 'discrimination is the simplest and most basic operation performable' (Stevens, in Cherry, 1957, p. 168). Life of itself, the brute stuff of Nature, cannot be held, after Darwin, to be exempt from the process of selection and, indeed, cyberneticians have been known to move from studies of feedback in machines to a view of natural organisms as maintaining themselves by the same process.[2] All this, however, has no direct effect on the human selector: 'the stimuli received from Nature – the sights and sounds – are not pictures of reality but are the evidence from which we build our personal models, or impressions, of reality'. Observing Nature is not communicating with her. When as scientists we observe her, she is 'uncooperative in the sense that she does not select the signs to suit our particular difficulties of observation at any time' (Cherry, 1957, p. 62).

Put another way: Nature, of and by herself, is continuous, whereas the human selector, precisely by selecting, sets up discontinuous patterns which stand out against her continuity much as a message in a certain code stands out against random noise in the atmosphere. You will gather from the example of a cocktail party that the more noise there is, the more people are likely to have to repeat themselves (sometimes in different ways) to get their message across. Thus (i) a message stands out discontinuously against random noise and (ii) the more interference there is from noise, the more *redundancy* is needed by the message.

Lévi-Strauss's arena is set where Nature and what he calls Culture overlap: he looks for the most basic processes which change natural man into cultural man and, in his early work, this was essentially a tripartite communication process in the exchange of goods, language, and women. In his new work, cultural man stands out on a background of Nature by virtue of his carved-out communication systems. This implies that his codes: goods, language, and women, if you like, are probably 'saying the same thing' – an implication not entirely new to anthropology, whether we look at *'le fait social total'* of Mauss, the 'culture pattern' idea, or the field of 'social relations'. Here I may be pushing Lévi-Strauss a little out of his own line, but we may be able to say that the various codes are in some senses redundant.

In some senses only, of course, since one cannot talk a table or make love to a language. But what of things which seem less discrete, such as, for instance, telling a myth and enacting a ritual? Here I seem to read in Lévi-Strauss that while myth and ritual may be saying the same thing, they are saying it on different levels and in such a way that complementariness or extra explication may result. Thus, after selection against noise, there may be a secondary selection against redundancy, giving room for variation and balance among overlapping cultural elements. This brings us to the important notion of transformation.

Playing games with code symbols is unique to man and the basis of all arts and sciences. The fertility of particular mathematical and logical statements or scientific experiments is measured by their power to generate transformations: i.e. further statements corresponding rigorously to the first statement but opening the way for comparison with other statements which were not, at first, held to be in the same field. Let us take a simple example: it is less useful for us to know that 1/4, 3/8, and 5/16ths are as they are than it is for us, in certain contexts, to know that the first two can be transformed into 4/16ths and 6/16ths. Now, in that part of *La Pensée sauvage* which has also appeared as 'The Bear and the Barber' (Lévi-Strauss, 1963b), Lévi-Strauss, by transforming, is able to propose some startling correspondences between totemic groups and castes which no one had ever thought of as being in the same field before. The notion of transformation is obviously very closely related to that of classification, for here it is our whole system of social anthropological classification which comes under fire.

Neither primitives nor social scientists, of course, waited for metalanguage to begin classification. Durkheim and Mauss (1903) showed, *inter alia*, that with such phenomena as totemism we are in the realm of taxonomy, a realm shared by Western scientist and primitive colleague alike, since both refer to species, classes, or groups. Now the creation of such a group is less simple than it appears. In *Figure 1*, the eight letters A-H

FIGURE 1. Two examples of Binary Coding by successive selection (adapted from Cherry, 1957, pp. 171, 228). The starred item would read: 1001.

Sign	Selections		
	1st	2nd	3rd
A	1	1	1
B	1	1	0
C	1	0	1
D	1	0	0
E	0	1	1
F	0	1	0
G	0	0	1
H	0	0	0

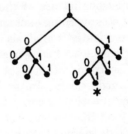

can, from the point of view of this binary coding, be divided into two sub-classes and four sub-sub-classes before getting down to individual units at the third selection. But what of a continuous wave form one wanted to code in telecommunication engineering? Here one would have to introduce the 'quantum', i.e. 'an interval on a scale of measurement, fractions of which

are considered to be of no significance' (Cherry, 1957, pp. 76 and
305). All taxonomy is to a greater or lesser extent a quantized
system. It is not entirely so in the case, say, of birds and
animals, where species are fairly clearly discontinuous, yet
what do we say, after centuries of miscegenation, of the human
race? We are aware, in sociology, of the many adjustments of
scale which take place in different multi-racial societies and
how these shift from society to society. All the more shall we
expect shifts in, say, the classification of animals and plants
when the criteria for classification may be so abstruse to our
own culture that we can hardly tell why certain natural elements
are, or are not, part of one class in the indigenous mind. If,
then, there is a degree of quantization in all taxonomy, we
find ourselves once again faced with the discontinuity of
the cultural process against the background of continuous
Nature.

The first chapter of *La Pensée sauvage* is a hymn of praise to
the breadth of primitive knowledge about Nature as revealed
in recent studies of ethnobotany and ethnozoology and in such
extensive world-view studies as Marcel Griaule's. This marks
a change of emphasis in Lévi-Strauss's work. In the period
of *Anthropologie structurale* (1958), he located the systematic
aspect of structure at the unconscious level of culture. The
unconscious nature of the level on which could be discovered
the laws governing exchange was the guarantee of the efficacity
of the scientist's analysis in that it safeguarded the study from
interference on his own part with the phenomena observed as
well as from rationalizations on the part of the people who
displayed them. Impressed by conscious knowledge and
communication theory, Lévi-Strauss seems to lay less stress
today on the unconscious level. Yet the basic premise has not
changed: there is that in human thought, at whatever level, in
whatever mind – be it the Australian aborigine's or the Collège
de France professor's – which gives unity to human thought
and it is simply the universal way in which the human mind
is constrained to work. If Freud and linguistics were the link
before, we now have the computer and the model of the brain.[3]
There is thus no end to the dialectic of readjustment of taxonomy; even the scientist is perpetually poised on the brink of

readjustment until that moment (in infinity?) when regions of uncertainty are no longer reducible. The fact is that scientific evidence for universal psychic unity *is* accumulating and Lévi-Strauss's hypotheses must appear of the same nature to him as did Freud's while he awaited biological confirmation of his. Winking at the cat at the end of *Tristes Tropiques* means that, if everything is play of mind, the greatest fun in life comes from possessing one of the century's best players.

Lévi-Strauss's insistence that only the model level belongs to science should now be clearly understood. From Locke to Peirce, the lesson is that we can have no true knowledge of the external world – all that we can affirm or deny about it is a matter of *probability*, an act of 'presumptive trust'. Knowledge consists in the perception of relations between ideas; true knowledge lies only in the agreement or disagreement of ideas. The extensive development of 'pure' systems in which *only* relations are known, in which we do not need to know what the fundamental concepts are but only how they could be related, strikes back at any intuition of fundamentals we may think we have and leads us into a world in which nothing exists of its own right but only as it is related to something else, in which every sign requires another to interpret it. This is perhaps another way of making Burridge's point about the interminable dialogue between the mind and its object and his reference to the last chapter of *La Pensée sauvage* where analysis is taken as being contained *in*, indeed as *being*, the dialectic.

I would like to clinch this with a quotation from an earlier work of Lévi-Strauss which strikes me as a further illustration of Burridge's description of a dilemma in Lévi-Strauss's thought resolved by some kind of universal participation in Nature.[4]

'It is in the relational character of symbolic thought that we can find the answer to our problem. Whatever may have been the time or the circumstances of its appearance in the scale of animal life, language could only have been brought to birth all at once. Things could not possibly have set themselves to signifying progressively. Following upon a transformation which it is not the Social Sciences' business to study, but Biology's and Psychology's, a passage took

125

place from a stage in which nothing had meaning to another in which everything had. Now this remark, however banal it may at first appear, is of importance because this radical change has no counterpart in the domain of knowledge, which elaborates itself only slowly and progressively. In other words, at the moment in which the whole Universe, in one fell stroke, became significant, it did not follow from this that it was any the better known; even if it is true that the appearance of language was to precipitate the rhythm of the development of knowledge.

Thus, there is, in the history of the human mind, a fundamental opposition between symbolism, with its character of discontinuity, and knowledge, characterized by continuity. The result is that the two categories of the signifying and the signified were constituted simultaneously and in reciprocal solidarity (*simultanément et solidairement*), like two complementary blocks, but that knowledge, i.e. the intellectual process which permits us to identify in respect of each other certain aspects of the signifying and certain aspects of the signified – one could even say: to choose from the entity of the signified those parts which present one towards another the most satisfactory relationship of mutual convenience – only set itself in motion very slowly. Everything happened as if humanity had acquired all at once an immense domain and the detailed plans thereof, together with the notion of their reciprocal relationship, but that it had spent thousands of years in order to learn which of the plan's determined symbols represented which different aspects of the domain.

The Universe was significant a long time before we began to find out what it signified; that much is obvious. But the preceding analysis also shows that it has signified, from the beginning, the totality of that which mankind can know of it. That which we call progress of the human mind and, in any case, the progress of scientific knowledge, has never consisted of, and never will consist of, more than a correction of outlines and classifications, a regrouping of elements, a definition of affiliations, and a discovery of new resources within an entity which is both closed and self-complementary' (1950, pp. xlvii-xlviii) [Mendelson's translation].[4]

The foregoing may serve as an introduction to *Le Totémisme aujourd'hui*, which is in turn an introduction to the much longer *La Pensée sauvage*. In this paper little more can be done than to account for the first.

If I have dwelt at length with new attitudes to the problem of taxonomy, it is because Lévi-Strauss considers our category of 'totemism' as a false one. For him, the 'totemic illusion' is the product of a late nineteenth- and early twentieth-century effort by scientists to relegate the primitive outside the realm of Culture. The term *Naturvölker* best betrays an effort to protect the Victorian world-view by maintaining the Christian distinction between man and Nature.[5] By failing, consciously or unconsciously, to recognize the similarities between Western and primitive codes, scholars created false taxonomies and blurred the universal logic behind all so-called 'totemic' phenomena. Discussion on Totemism rapidly became an industry among anthropologists, reaching its apogee with Van Gennep, but it contained from the start the seeds of its own disintegration. In 1910, Goldenweiser, in 110 pages, cracked open Frazer's 2,200 pages by pointing out that there was no necessary link between (i) clan organization, (ii) clan attribution of animal or vegetal emblems, and (iii) a belief in kinship relations between clan and emblem. For Lévi-Strauss, two basic problems have been confused: (i) that which deals with the frequent identification of humans with non-human things and belongs to the wider problem of man's relations to Nature and (ii) that which deals with the description of kinship groups by the use of animal-vegetal terms, but also in many other ways. The word 'totem' would occur only when these two orders coincide or overlap. Now, it is true that any form of kinship group exogamy involving a formal structure reaching beyond consanguine ties and needing an unequivocal set of filiation rules and name-transmission through filiation is a requisite of any totemic system. But recourse to animal/vegetal names is only a particular case of a method of differential name-ascription whose structural characteristics are of one formal type whatever the denotation system may be. Why, then, are the animal and vegetal worlds called upon?

They 'are not utilized merely because they are there, but because they suggest a mode of thought. The connection between the *relation of man to nature* and the *characterization of social groups*, which Boas thought to be contingent and arbitrary, only seems so because the real link between the two orders is indirect, passing through the mind. This postulates a homology, not so much within the system of denotation, but between differential features existing, on the one hand, between species x and y, and, on the other, between clan a and clan b' (Lévi-Strauss, 1962a, p. 18; 1964a, p. 13).

The method followed to study the logical power of denotation systems (already noted by Tylor in 1899 but never developed) is the structural model method, the model to include all possible permutations between the structure's terms. In *Figure 2*

FIGURE 2. The four permutations of the 'Totemic Illusion' model (see Lévi-Strauss, 1962a, pp. 23-24; 1964a, pp. 16-17).

		1	2	3	4
Binary Antithesis	Nature	CATEGORY	CATEGORY	INDIVIDUAL	INDIVIDUAL
	Culture	GROUP	PERSON	PERSON	GROUP
Lévi-Strauss's examples		Sex totems and social totems in Australia	Individual totems among North American Indians	Single animal incarnation, Mota (Bank's Island); also Algonquin Indians	Species animals as sacred emblems. (New Zealand, Africa, Egypt, Siberia)

totemism covers ideological relations postulated between two series, one natural, one cultural; each with two modes, collective and individual. This generates four permutations, each ascribable to field examples – though numbers 3 and 4 were excluded by the 'totemic illusion'. In other terms, the illusion distorted the semantic field by an inefficient selection of elements which, by concentrating on 1 and 2, made 1 and 2 more mysterious than they really are.[6]

Let us follow Lévi-Strauss for a moment on permutations

1 and 2. An Ojibwa refers to himself as a clansman in terms from which the word *totem* is derived and which involve a category of animals. The terminology which refers to an Ojibwa individual's personal relationship with an animal guardian spirit is quite distinct from the 'totemic' terminology. One can show that the first description of supposed totemism resulted from a confusion of these terminologies: one Lévi-Strauss calls 'social', in which animal names correspond to *collective* appellations, the other, 'religious', in which animal guardian-spirits are *individual* protectors (description by Long, 1791). Ojibwa did not believe clan members to be descended from the totemic animal, nor was the latter the object of a cult. When new social types – crossbreeds – had to be fitted in, they were classified under European animals, such as fowl or pig. While totemic clan names were co-equivalent (horizontal one might say), guardian spirits were strongly hierarchized (vertical). Food taboos pertained to spirits only, being revealed to individuals at the apex of their quest. Totemic species, however, could be freely killed and eaten by their clansmen. Lévi-Strauss surmises that Long's confusion was probably due to the guardian spirit's never being 'a particular mammal or bird, such as one might see by day around the wigwam, but a supernatural being which represented the whole species'.

Turning to Tikopia, Lévi-Strauss observes that Firth's data require a third axis (additional to the group-individual and Nature-Culture ones) on which should be arranged the different conceivable types of relation between the extreme terms of the first two: emblematic, relations of identity, descent or interest, direct, indirect, etc. These are expressed in another fundamental opposition between a 'social' totemic system focused on plants and a 'religious' system focused on animals. Each of the four clans, or their chiefs, controls one of four basic plants, but three express their relation through rituals, the fourth through prohibitions and prescription. Now, the plants are held to be sacred because they 'represent' the gods.[7] Turning to animals, we find that the category of edible things which includes the four plants also includes edible fish. There is no association of clans and edible fish. On the other hand, the gods are said 'to be' (not 'to represent') fish and *these* turn out to belong to

129

the category of inedible things, thus excluding the edible things from *being* gods. There is more than this, but we have enough to discern, as among Ojibwa, radical differences between permutations 1 and 2, as well as certain overlapping factors which gave rise to the 'totemic illusion'. Firth is quoted as concluding that totemism does not constitute a phenomenon *sui generis* but a specific instance in the general field of relations between man and the objects of his natural environment.[8]

The Maori constitute 'a limiting case which permits the distinction, in a pure state, of categories which are mutually exclusive but which the totemic hypothesis would have to say were compatible' (Lévi-Strauss, 1962a, pp. 42-43; 1964a, p. 30). In Maori cosmology, everything is related – the world is a vast kinship system. 'Now if the natural beings or elements are related to each other as ancestors to descendants, and all of them are so related to mankind, then none is fit in itself to play the part of ancestor in relation to any particular human group' (*idem*). In other words, the Maori monogenetic system excludes the polygenesis of totemism, or, again, 'true' or 'real' ancestors exclude 'false' or 'symbolic' totems. I shall return to all this later on.

I must sketch the rest in less detail. The order in which various theories, mainly British, accede to the Lévi-Straussian light runs roughly as follows: Malinowski and Radcliffe-Brown (1929) through Elkin, Firth, Fortes, Evans-Pritchard, and, finally, Radcliffe-Brown's second theory of 1951. The argument from 'needs' – that objects are selected as totems because they are particularly useful or economically significant – is rapidly dismissed by examining negative instances. Malinowski is guilty of operating almost entirely within the world of Nature and his theory leaves us to explain why totemism, if it responds to human 'needs', is not universal. (Conversely Durkheim suffers from operating entirely within the world of Culture, albeit with a touch of psychology in his 'social effervescence' notion.) Radcliffe-Brown's earlier idea that objects become totems because they are of ritual interest to society can be turned round: why are they not of ritual interest because they have been designated as totems?

Firth and Fortes accomplished great progress in passing from theories based on subjective utility to theories based on objective analogy. They pointed out that natural species were not *arbitrarily* selected as totemic badges. Furthermore, the fact of selection did not necessarily imply that any relation, such as descent or predication of any certain common quality, automatically existed between the totem and the person or group who acknowledged it. On the contrary, it was felt that an elucidation of the 'meaning' of a totem in its symbolic context, followed by a demonstration of the relevance of this connotation for the group or person which acknowledged the totem, was necessary for the understanding of the links binding the group or person to their eponym. This contextualization, however, had the unfortunate effect of causing the understanding of the question to be too much related to contingent circumstances particular to the societies involved, thus making them recalcitrant to generalization. In any case a further point of importance was involved:

'If we may be allowed the expression, *it is not the resemblances, but the differences, which resemble each other.* By this we mean that there are not, first, animals which resemble each other (because they all share animal behaviour), then ancestors which resemble each other (because they all share ancestral behaviour), and lastly an overall resemblance between the two groups; but on the one hand there are animals which differ from each other (in that they belong to distinct species, each of which has its own physical appearance and mode of life), and on the other there are men – among whom the ancestors form a particular case – who also differ from each other (in that they are distributed among different segments of the society, each occupying a particular position in the social structure). The resemblance presupposed by so-called totemic representations is *between these two systems of differences.* Firth & Fortes have taken a great step in passing from a point of view centered on *subjective utility* to one of *objective analogy.* But, this progress having been made, it remains to effect the passage from *external analogy* to *internal homology*' (Lévi-Strauss, 1962a, p. 111; 1964a, p. 77).

The remaining step is derived from Evans-Pritchard and Radcliffe-Brown (1951) where the question is, for instance, not 'Why all these birds?' but 'Why particularly Eaglehawk and Crow amongst other pairs?' Selection by natives implies that they are thought of as being in a relation of opposition along a common dimension: thus both are meat-eaters, but the Eagle is hunter, the Crow scavenger. This difference serves to distinguish human groups so that E : C :: moiety A : moiety B – or one human group is to another human group as one species is to another, i.e. discrete. We arrive at a very common structural principle: the complementariness of opposite pairs, another example of a binary-type discrimination.

'The alleged Totemism is no more than a particular expression, by means of a special nomenclature formed of animal and plant names (in a certain code, as we should say today), which is its sole distinctive characteristic, of correlations and oppositions which may be formalized in other ways, e.g. among certain tribes of North and South America, by oppositions of the type sky/earth, war/peace, upstream/downstream, red/white, etc. The most general model of this, and the most systematic application, is to be found perhaps in China, in the opposition of the two principles of Yang and Yin, as male and female, day and night, summer and winter, the union of which results in an organized totality (*tao*) such as the conjugal pair, the day, or the year. Totemism is thus reduced to a particular fashion of formulating a general problem, viz. how to make opposition, instead of being an obstacle to integration, serve rather to produce it.

Radcliffe-Brown's demonstration ends decisively the dilemma in which the adversaries as well as the proponents of Totemism have been trapped because they could assign only two roles to living species, viz., that of natural stimulus, or that of an arbitrary pretext. The animals in Totemism cease to be solely or principally creatures which are feared, admired or envied: their perceptible reality permits the embodiment of ideas and relations conceived by speculative thought on the basis of empirical observation. We can understand, too, that natural species are chosen not because

they are "good to eat" but because they are "good to think" '
(Lévi-Strauss, 1962a, p. 127; 1964a, p. 89).

In the final chapter, Lévi-Strauss shows the unexpected and
surprising congruence of Bergson, Jean Jacques Rousseau, and
Radcliffe-Brown. Bergson, he argues, understood primitive
thought so well because his own doctrine of creative evolution
was so close to certain modes of primitive thought (Sioux
examples). The kinship is described by Lévi-Strauss as resulting

'from one and the same desire to apprehend in a total
fashion the two aspects of reality which the philosopher terms
continuous and *discontinuous*; from the same refusal to
choose between the two; and from the same effort to see
them as complementary perspectives giving on to the same
truth. Radcliffe-Brown, though abstaining from metaphysical
considerations which were foreign to his temperament,
followed the same route, when he reduced Totemism to a
particular form of a universal tendency, in order to reconcile
opposition and *integration*' (Lévi-Strauss, 1962a, p. 141;
1964a, pp. 98-99).

Durkheim, on the other hand, while fully aware, in the
classification theory which was to be so fertile in Mauss's hands,
of the intellect's role in social life, paralysed himself by his
affirmation that the social primes over the intellectual. While
Bergson can make of intellectual categories immediate data of
the mind utilized by the social order to define and constitute
itself, Durkheim, tying intellect to social forms, is left with a
highly impoverished field of explanatory elements with which
to account for the social order. He must thus fall back on
sentiments, affective values, and vague ideas of contamination
and contagion.

Yet more of a master of the passage from Nature to Culture
was Rousseau, writing in complete ignorance of totemism, that
is before Long's contribution. Rousseau is hailed by Lévi-
Strauss as having grasped the triple passage from animality to
humanity, Nature to Culture, and affectivity to intellectuality
through the medium of the only psychic human state whose
content is indissociably both affective and intellectual – the

passage being made automatically as soon as man is conscious of being in this state. The state is *pitié*, compassion, or identification with alterity, the duality of terms corresponding up to a point with the duality of appearances. For it is because we have first seen our identity with all other beings through *pitié* and identification that we can then distinguish ourselves from others; because we have apprehended similarity between two terms that we can also apprehend differences. We are back to metaphor seen, not as a late embellishment of language (Rousseau's thought was prophetic of modern structural linguistics), but as one of its fundamental modes.

I have little time left in which to illustrate some of my difficulties. I believe this seminar is going to agree that Lévi-Strauss is highly exciting but that he must move so quickly over so large a terrain that doubts arise as soon as one is out of the centre of the light he throws. That, and a tendency to rhetoric in which categories sometimes sideslip alarmingly.[9] Provided we are un-British enough to raise three cheers for sheer achievement, niggling doubts such as the following might now no doubt be entertained.

My Ojibwa/Tikopia/Maori examples were taken from Chapter 1 of Lévi-Strauss, 1962a, which is also the locus of many of my difficulties. Observing, in passing, the doubtful appearance of a 'social' *v.* 'religious' terminological pair, I dwell on one passage which I must quote in detail:

'These Indians [Ojibwa] were, it seems, organized into some dozens of patrilineal and patrilocal clans, of which five *may have been* older than the others, or, at any rate, enjoyed a particular prestige. A myth explains that these five "original" clans are descended from six anthropomorphic supernatural beings who emerged from the ocean to mingle with human beings. One of them had his eyes covered and dared not look at the Indians, though he showed the greatest anxiety to do so. At last he could no longer restrain his curiosity, and on one occasion he partially lifted his veil, and his eye fell on the form of a human being, who instantly fell dead "as if struck by one of the thunderers". Though the intentions of this dread being were friendly to men, yet the glance of his

eye was too strong, and it inflicted certain death. His fellows
therefore caused him to return to the bosom of the waters.
The five others remained among the Indians, and "became a
blessing to them". From them originate the five great clans
or totems: catfish, crane, loon, bear and marten.

In spite of the *mutilated form* in which it has been handed
down to us, this myth is of considerable interest. It affirms,
to begin with, that there can be no direct relationship, based
on contiguity, between man and totem. The only possible
relationship must be "masked", *and thus* metaphorical, as is
confirmed by the fact, reported from Australia and America,
that the totemic animal is *sometimes* designated by another
name than that applied to the real animal, to the extent that
the clan name does not immediately and normally arouse a
zoological or botanical association in the native mind.

In the second place, the myth establishes another opposition, between personal relation and collective relation. The
Indian does not die just *because* he is looked at, but *also*
because of the singular behaviour of one of the supernatural
beings, whereas the others act with more discretion, and as a
group' (Lévi-Strauss, 1962a, p. 26; 1964a, pp. 19-20) (my
italics).

The distinction between 'the five' and 'No. 6' is not as clear
as one might wish. It might be argued that action of the latter
is but a logical projection of that of the former: they had all
come to *mingle* with men: you can't mingle while being blind
all the time and 'No. 6' actually did *look*. Further, we are told
nothing about 'the five' positively, only that they did not do
what 'No. 6' did. It could be read that 'the five' are *not* masked
('*one of them* had his eyes covered'), yet it would seem desirable
for Lévi-Strauss's opposition that they should be. Finally there
would seem to be some redundancy in the duplication of
because in the Lévi-Strauss last sentence: the looking *is* the
singular behaviour.

The phrase 'The only possible relationship must be "masked",
and thus metaphorical' is problematical. The contiguity/
metonymy and similarity/metaphor pair of distinctions which
play such an important role in these difficult pages refer to an

important aspect of Jakobson's work on two polar figures of speech. Briefly metaphor is based on the *substitution* of one distinctive feature of language for another (characteristic of poetry) while metonymy is based on the *contiguity* of two distinctive features (characteristic of prose). The reference here is mainly to the lexical, syntactic, and phraseological levels, though one can go down to the morphemic level in the aphasia brain lesions which revealed the importance of these polar types'. 'Contiguity disorder' alienates metonymy in speech, 'similarity disorder' alienates metaphor (see Jakobson & Halle, 1956, pp. 55-82). Now, I do not see clearly how a 'metaphorical' relation can be said to be either more or less *masked* than a metonymic one. It may be that a second term substituted for a first 'masks' the first whereas a contiguous second term merely *follows* a first term which retains its position in the message. On the other hand, such a contiguous term does not *'unmask'* the first, it merely follows it. Here: what is masking what?

Lévi-Strauss argues that 'No. 6' tells us something about the Guardian Spirit as opposed to the Totem. But – does a Guardian Spirit kill the man he protects? We are not told, yet if the killing is initiatic (i.e. merely the prelude to life-enhancement) Lévi-Strauss's previous *killing* stuff is unconvincing. Another question is: how often does an individual in fact get a protector who also happens to belong to a totemic species? We are not told; is it impossible?

In my very tentative *Figure 1*, the metaphor/metonymy opposition blossoms out into a proliferation of others. In Lévi-Strauss (1962a, pp. 26-27; 1964a, pp. 36-37) metaphor is linked with similarity and resemblance (which fit the *substitution* requirement) and with discontinuity as opposed to the continuity of metonymic relations. At the same time we are told – when reference is made to the incarnating gods of Tikopia versus the vegetal totems – that the relation between totem and god is of a more *permanent* nature than the relation between god and occasional animal into which the god incarnates. Now 'permanent' has, to my mind, the sense of continuity – yet here we are dealing with the *discontinuous* metaphorical relation of totemism. Vocabulary is a little strained in these dense pages.

The 'Uninvited Guest'

The patience comes out well in the Maori case. Associating metaphor with 'social Totem' and metonymy with 'religious spirit or god', Lévi-Strauss proposes another pair extension: 'one might almost say that metonymy corresponds to the order

FIGURE 3. Tentative attempt to show graphically a number of binary discriminations by Lévi-Strauss, as discussed in *Le Totémisme aujourd'hui*.

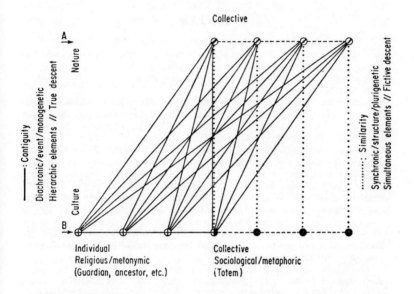

of events, metaphor to the order of structure' (1962a, p. 38; 1964a, p. 27). This is clinched, in the case of the historical ancestor versus the non-historical Totem by the argument that metonymy fits with the detailed illustration of every historical link in the chain from first ancestor to lowest descendant in a monogenetic system. Metaphor, on the other hand, cannot illustrate every link: in a polygenetic system (such as totemism) the cards are all laid on the table in one go: no cards are held in reserve to illustrate the stages of transition between the animal/vegetal ancestor and the human descendant. The passage from one to another is thus necessarily conceived as discontinuous (all transitions of the same type, moreover, being simultaneous), a veritable scene-shifting, without dropping the

137

curtain, which excludes all perceptible contiguity between the initial and final stages. The analysis of totemism can thus well be said to belong to an 'ethnologic'. It follows that in my *Figure 1* the broken lines relating Category to Group on the right imply no time passage between the Nature and Culture levels, whereas the continuous lines on the left do imply such a passage in the relation of Category to Person.

NOTES

1. Jakobson and Halle (1956, pp. 29-31). We can define phonemes as 'a minimal list of phonetic elements with which it is possible to represent and to distinguish one word from another in a language'.
2. Feedback: the setting-up of self-stabilizing control action by an effect retroacting upon one of its factors.
3. An excellent short account of the cross-fertilization of disciplines – in this case Communication Engineering and Neurology – occurs in John von Neumann's *The Computer and the Brain* (1958). Lévi-Strauss's interest in von Neumann's work is well known.
4. The praise of Buddhism which occurs in the last chapters of *Tristes Tropiques* may also be elucidated by the curious equation here between an 'essence' which has been there from the beginning '*in toto*' and an 'existence' which merely reveals its plan in history. One is also reminded of the 'self's' painful discovery of its original condition through the mind's more and more exasperated efforts to break down all possible contradictions.
5. Sacrifice also blurred this distinction but could not be dismissed as entirely primitive since it was obviously a part of the Western higher religions. By linking *natur* totemism to *natur* sacrifice, however, primitive sacrifice could be to some extent kept in its place.
6. 'Inefficient selection of elements': 'un mauvais découpage de la realité' (Lévi-Strauss, 1962a, p. 25) [Needham translates this as 'a mistaken division of reality' (1964a, p. 18) E.R.L.].
7. Yam: body of Kafika; taro: body of Taumako; breadfruit: head of Fangarere; coconut: head of Tafua.
8. Further contrasts between totems and gods are revealed by the fact that the god is believed to enter the fish but does not change into it; it is never the totality of the species that is in question but only a single animal; the occurrence is exceptional whereas the relations between clans and plants are permanent. A number of religious, non-totemic prohibitions are associated with the fact that the god can incarnate a number of different animals.
9. An example is provided by the long quotation from Lévi-Strauss (1950) cited above. In view of most of what has been said in this paper, it is a little hard to see 'knowledge' as '*continuous*'.

REFERENCES

CHERRY, C. 1957. *On Human Communication*. Cambridge, Mass.: M.I.T. Press. (Paperback edition 1961. New York: Science Editions.)

The 'Uninvited Guest'

DURKHEIM, E. & MAUSS, M. 1903. De quelques formes primitives de classification: contribution a l'étude des réprésentations collectives. Paris: *L'Année sociologique* **6**: 1-72 (English translation, 1963. *Primitive Classification*. London: Cohen & West).

GOLDENWEISER, A. A. 1910. Totemism: An Analytical Study. *Journal of American Folklore* **23**: 179-293. Reprinted with modifications in A. A. Goldenweiser. 1933. *History, Psychology & Culture*. London: Kegan Paul.

JAKOBSON, R. & HALLE, K. 1956. *Fundamentals of Language*. The Hague: Mouton.

LÉVI-STRAUSS, C. 1950. Introduction à l'oeuvre de Marcel Mauss. In M. Mauss, *Sociologie et anthropologie*. Paris: Presses Universitaires de France, pp. ix-lii.

―― 1955a. *Tristes Tropiques* (English translation, 1961. *A World on the Wane*. London: Hutchinson.)

―― 1958a. *Anthropologie structurale*. Paris: Plon. (English translation, 1963a. *Structural Anthropology*. New York: Basic Books.)

―― 1962a. *Le Totémisme aujourd'hui*. (English translation, 1964a. *Totemism*. London: Merlin Press.)

―― 1962b. *La Pensée sauvage*. Paris: Plon.

―― 1963b. The Bear and the Barber. *Journal of the Royal Anthropological Institute* **93**: Part I, 1-11.

LONG, J. 1791. *Voyages & Travels of an Indian Interpreter*. London. (Reprinted in J. Long, 1922. *John Long's Voyages & Travels in the years 1768-1788*. Chicago: R. R. Donnelly & Sons.)

RADCLIFFE-BROWN, A. R. 1929. The Sociological Theory of Totemism. *Proceedings of Fourth Pacific Science Congress*, Java. Reprinted in A. R. Radcliffe-Brown, 1952. *Structure & Function in Primitive Society*. London: Cohen & West.

―― 1951. The Comparative Method in Social Anthropology. *Journal of the Royal Anthropological Institute* **81**: 15-22. Reprinted in A. R. Radcliffe-Brown, 1958. *Method in Social Anthropology*. Chicago: University of Chicago Press.

VON NEUMANN, J. 1958. *The Computer and the Brain*. New Haven: Yale University Press.

Peter Worsley

Groote Eylandt Totemism and
Le Totémisme aujourd'hui

'Thought which is totally unscientific and even which contradicts
experience may yet be entirely coherent in that there is a reciprocal dependence between its ideas. Thus I may instance the
writings of medieval divines and political controversialists as
examples of mystical thought which, far from being chaotic,
suffers from a too rigid application of syllogistic rules. Also the
thought of many insane persons (monomaniacs, paranoiacs)
presents a perfectly organized system of interdependent ideas.'
                              E. E. EVANS-PRITCHARD (1934, p. 51)

'The insane have a terrific obsession for logic and order, as have
the French.'
                              HENRY MILLER (1936)

The two quotations at the head of this article only refer
obliquely – and most affectionately – to the writing of that
most respected and creative of colleagues, Claude Lévi-Strauss;
they bear more centrally upon the thinking of the Australian
aborigines. I have no desire, that is, to be cast in the role of a
simple-minded English empiricist breaking a lance for God,
Harry, and the Cult of the Fact against the dragon of Gallic
systematics. Even though the orientation of this paper was
originally suggested to me as the presentation of Australian
aboriginal totemism 'as it really is', such a 'pure' empiricist
brief is logically impossible, for 'as it really is' (shades of
Ranke!) has to be translated 'as it really is *in contradistinction
to Lévi-Strauss's interpretations*'. As Lévi-Strauss would no
doubt be the first to observe, an analysis of totemism 'as it
really is' cannot exist 'in itself', but implies its opposite.

Yet I may 'revise' the Marxian dialectic this far: that I do
not conceive of my arguments as being any kind of 'antithesis'
to Lévi-Strauss's 'thesis'. The analysis here develops, not in
negative *o*pposition to his approach, but in *a*pposition to it.
Any discussion of totemism must be conditioned by his signifi-

cant contribution to our understanding of the phenomenon: it must extend his insights.

Simple empiricism, indeed, invites the kind of criticism that Lévi-Strauss develops in discussing Elkin's fragmentation of 'totemism' into various 'totemisms': sex totemism, moiety totemism, clan totemism, dream totemism, local totemisms, section totemism, sub-section totemism, etc. (Elkin, 1933). The problem is merely rephrased, not eliminated: now it becomes 'What is the sociological significance of totemism*s*', instead of 'What is the sociological significance of totemism?'

Or, as Lévi-Strauss wittily puts it, Elkin, 'instead of helping to slay the hydra [of totemism] . . . has dismembered it and made peace with the bits' (Lévi-Strauss, 1962a, p. 66).

For Lévi-Strauss, indeed, the problem is not to understand totemism, but to abolish it. Totemism is not a separable 'ethnographic' specimen peculiar to the Australians and some other peoples, but a particular instance of a much more general phenomenon, one indeed that all societies have to face in one way or another: the problem of how men perceive, select, intellectually order, and socially structure the similarities and differences in both the natural and cultural realms respectively, and how connections are established between these two orders. It is not that there is a 'natural' order in Nature, which, as in seventeenth-century theories of consciousness, somehow 'orders' or registers itself automatically within brains which passively 'receive' these already-processed sense impressions. Nature itself is ordered by the *active* organizing intervention of the brain, as the eighteenth-century idealists, notably Kant, correctly told us. The order of Nature is not mechanically registered, but is created by human agency. It is an ordering achieved via human consciousness, not an order 'in itself'.[1] The ordering of Nature is thus as much a human product, the outcome of human activity within Nature, as is (more obviously) the ordering of society. The gulf between verbal and non-verbal aspects of culture, between the ordering of cultural experience through the medium of written documents and ordering via the classification of other objects in the environment is thus bridged in Lévi-Strauss's analysis. The totemic 'objects are not just *objects*; they are messages'[2] (Lévi-Strauss, 1962b, p. 355).

In classifying, man organizes his experience, and locates the classified raw materials of his experience within a framework of *meaning*; the imputation of meaning rests upon an underlying set of values. Thus the worlds of natural objects and cultural objects are brought into relationship with each other. In Lévi-Strauss's paradoxical formulation, the problem then consists in analysing how these *differences* between the two areas, Nature and Culture, 'resemble' each other (or perhaps, more accurately, 'are brought into relationship'), since there may not be – as we shall see – that closeness of fit between different classificatory schemes within the same culture which alone would permit us, legitimately, to speak of 'resemblance', 'congruence', etc.[3]

One possible type of explanation of totemism rejected by Lévi-Strauss (1962a, Ch. 5) is the naturalistic or utilitarian type, which asserts that the objects selected as totems are so selected because of their usefulness, normally as food or in terms of some other economic 'good' (e.g. as raw materials, etc.). This he rejects, since, on the one hand (to take animals used as totems), many animals found in the totemic schemata are not necessarily of much (if any) economic importance, and, moreover, by no means occupy a place in the ritual hierarchy which would correspond to their degree of importance from a utilitarian point of view. Thus, to take illustrations from the totems of one single clan of the Wanindiljaugwa tribe of Groote Eylandt, Northern Territory of Australia – whom I studied in 1953 as a Research Scholar of the Australian National University – parrot fish, dugong, paperbark, and cypress pine are all valued either as foods or as raw material, but the echidna, scrub fowl, goose, or crow are not so valued, either because they are not regarded as edible, or because they are rarely encountered. The presence of the Northwest wind as a further totem of this clan raises a problem, however, for clearly it is not used either for food or for raw material. One can argue that it is of 'economic' significance, either because it fills the sails of the aborigines' canoes, or – more convincingly – because this wind symbolizes the wet season of the year. But this argument involves such a radical extension of the notion of 'economic interest' from simple, specific, and direct utility in production

143

and consumption, to diffuse and symbolic 'social value', that it could be used to rationalize *anything* as having 'social value' (it also assumes what has to be proved – that the totemic entities are adopted *because* they 'reflect' some underlying concern with the utilitarian). The ultimate absurdity of this position is reached when we find things like diarrhoea, vomit, or the mosquito used as totems. How are these of 'social value'? The only possible way out of this is to argue that they are of 'negative social value', i.e. they are important because they are noxious. By this stage, since practically everything in society and Nature has either a positive or negative social value, we are still left with the problem of why *this* (often minor) item has been selected, and not that. Normally, however, it is not necessary to fall back on the argument from 'negative social value'. Since the aborigine has a prodigious knowledge of natural species, and uses hundreds of plants and animals, nearly every plant or animal which can possibly occur in a totemic collection can be shown to have at least some, partial or occasional, utility value.

The totems, then, are not necessarily of greater economic importance than are species of animals and plants which do not figure as totems. Many totems are not natural species at all; some of them are noxious; or, like the 'sleep' totem reported from one tribe, could perhaps be regarded as neutral, rather than either positive or negative.

Durkheim himself had originally pointed out that it was erroneous to interpret the function of totemism as the maintenance of valued plants and animals, when he observed that the so-called 'increase' rituals were also performed within the context of initiation (Durkheim, 1957, p. 384). Moreover, since the environment of the aborigines contains only an exiguous man-made culture, natural species are bound to predominate, merely because they are plentiful and accessible (though heavenly bodies, inorganic substances such as stones, and geographical features, are all totems which are natural, but not species).

If, then, certain animal and plant species (though, to be precise, aboriginal taxonomic divisions do not necessarily coincide with the biologist's *species*) are used as totems, it is not

144

because these species are *choses bonnes à manger*. But are they any less good to 'think with' than other 'failed' totems? Are they, in fact, just arbitrary symbols, only connected to the social units that bear them in a purely contingent way – say, through historical accident – which then become 'fixed', or are they more systematically distributed among the component social units according to consistent principles of distribution?

For some totemic systems, as in the analysis of Tallensi totemism by Fortes (1945, pp. 141-145), a peculiar appropriateness has been suggested for the animals used as totems (tooth-bearing animals which symbolize the potential aggressiveness of the ancestors). Malinowski and Firth, earlier, had suggested that animals were inherently more suitable totemic material than plants, because of their distinctive differences in motility, form, colour, sound, etc. (Lévi-Strauss, 1962a, pp. 82-83, 108-109).

But these modes of analysis, even if accepted as valid for the Tallensi and Tikopia, are not extensible beyond these societies. What is common to both types of explanation, however – which is extensible generally – is the observation which Lévi-Strauss found foreshadowed in Bergson (1958): that it is not the individual characteristics of particular animals that are highlighted in totemic classifications, but the *generic* characteristics of whole classes of animal.

Even this, however, is only relevant in so far as specifically *animal* totems are concerned. But not all totems are animal totems. And even among animal totems, in Australian totemism, species possessing negative, low, or marginal social value, or even those which are neutral in value terms, take their place together with species having a high positive value. The same applies to plant species.

One Groote Eylandt set of linked totems illustrates the difficulties entailed in naturalistic assumptions that the intrinsic characteristics of the totem 'explain' the social value placed upon it. In one of the Creation Time myths, the mythical creatures Dumaringenduma and Neribuwa occur, together with Parrot, Central Hill, and four or five sea-creatures: usually Saw-fish, Sting-ray, Comb-fish, and Shark-ray.

From a utilitarian point of view, parrots are by no means important, except periodically as a source of feathers for decorating the body. Central Hill, however, is the highest hill not only on Groote Eylandt, but also in the whole Gulf of Carpentaria – an obvious naturalistic explanation of its central importance in this myth. Again, Sting-ray's importance might well be said to derive, not so much from its considerable importance as a food, but from the striking resemblance in shape of Lake Hubert (the largest lake on the island), seen from a distance, to a sting-ray. Yet the latter is only an inference – Central Hill *is* a totem itself; Lake Hubert is not, but (to the observer, under certain conditions) looks like a sting-ray, and in the myth, Sting-ray ends his journey in this lake (but so do Saw-fish, Comb-fish, and Shark-ray!). One major topographical feature – Central Hill – clearly has high place in the totemic collection; so does Lake Hubert (though only if we assume that Lake Hubert = Sting-ray). But quite as important, to the aborigine, are two utterly insignificant rocks, in physical terms, which 'are' Neribuwa and Dumaringenduma (so insignificant, among dozens of others in the same hilly outcrop, that I was never sure which two the aborigines were pointing to). In this myth, then, anthropomorphic Dream Time Beings, topographical features possessed of a human-like volition and motility (Central Hill), and animals, all occur together and have similar status. But Neribuwa and Dumaringenduma *became* natural features; Central Hill is always depicted as a *hill* (in bark-paintings, Neribuwa and Dumaringenduma are shown as *people*). There is really little that is systematic here. It may well be that the four sea-creatures are selected for their sharp 'noses', for these four 'cut open' the Jinuma (Anggurgwa) River, the major river of Groote Eylandt. There appears to be no good utilitarian reason why a cottonwood tree should be connected with these other totems in the myth.

This myth thus 'explains' the largest hill, the largest lake, and the largest river on the island. (Other quite large lakes have no such myths attached to them.) The path of the journeys of the Dream Time creatures probably reflects something quite distinct: the major routes by which, historically, people have always moved from the mainland into Groote Eylandt.

All this makes some kind of systematic sense, much of it in utilitarian terms. Similarly, another myth 'explains', not topographical features, but the gulf between men and animals: it tells how man came to use fire in cooking fish (the word for fish – *augwalja* – interestingly enough, is extended to mean flesh-food in general), while the sea-eagle came to eat fish raw. To say this is to analyse the myth in terms of behaviours; not, simply, to assume that animals occurring in myths are of high utilitarian value (sea-eagles, garfish, and grasshoppers – all of which occur in the myth – are not so valued). Similarly, the Ship totemic myth-complex 'explains' not merely the technological item, ship, but also the division of humankind into aborigines and Makassarese (smoke from a fire turned the aborigines black; the Whites, however, are not totemically 'explained' at all).

As I have described elsewhere (1955, pp. 851-861, and 1956, pp. 47-62, though the latter article suffers from a far too naturalistic interpretation, which internal evidence does not support), other important aspects of aboriginal life – topographical features such as the major hill on neighbouring Bickerton Island (also inhabited by the Wanindiljaugwa), the winds which mark the seasons, the Ship totem – represent mythological celebration of key features of Groote Eylandt life. But there is no myth to celebrate, say, the spear-thrower or the axe, the grey mullet (an important fish-food), the dugout canoe, tobacco, night and day, the differential behaviours of men and women, or a hundred and one equally significant elements in the natural and cultural worlds. And a further myth (of another clan) celebrates a whole series of utterly insignificant places: it does include four practically important items (bark canoe, barbed spears, Southeast wind, and stringy-bark); lesser-valued items (casuarina tree); and various 'useless' items (caterpillar, praying mantis); and one that is, to me, inexplicable – 'place'.

To pursue systematics as far as one can, one may further observe one binary discrimination that appears an almost triumphant demonstration of mythological order: the largest clan in one moiety has the Northwest wind (wet season) as its key (most-frequently-mentioned) totem, and the largest clan in the other moiety the Southeast wind (dry season). The

147

North wind, which blows for a short time between the major seasons, is allotted to a smaller clan in the moiety which has the Northwest wind. Each moiety contains six clans. In moiety A, four clans share the same totemic complex; in moiety B, another four clans again share another complex.

This is all very orderly, until we examine how this order comes about. It would appear likely (conjectural history) that the two totemic myth complexes mentioned (the myth shared by four clans, involving Central Hill, Sting-ray, Dumaringen-duma, etc., and the Ship myth of four clans in the other moiety) embody actual migration-routes, as does the Southeast wind myth complex of the Wanindiljaugwa clan (Wanindil-jaugwa being the name both of the tribe as a whole and of a clan within the tribe). We do, however, have some probably historical material to hand. Two clans – the WanungAmadada and the WurEngiljangba, are said, quite specifically, by the aborigines, to be new formations, notably the former, much the larger of the two. This clan was 'produced' only one genera-tion ago by one, still-living, ritual expert from the Nunggubuju tribe on the mainland opposite, who immigrated to Groote Eylandt and adopted the totems of the WuraGwaugwa clan. He also became a Groote Eylandt ritual leader and introduced mainland rituals into Wanindiljaugwa practice. Totems and whole rituals have probably always been borrowed or intro-duced from the mainland and vice versa; today, the Wanindil-jaugwa seem to experience a distinct sense of ritual ignorance and inferiority *vis-à-vis* the mainlanders, whose flourishing and rich ritual life they envy; they are therefore accustomed to 'borrow' mainland rituals.

By the creation of two new clans, entirely – it appears – contingent upon a quite recent specific immigration (even allowing for possible 'telescoping', 'fusing', etc.), a spuriously neat balance of six clans in each moiety is achieved.

This mainland contact, recorded even in eighteenth-century exploration literature, has constantly fed new totems into Groote Eylandt. A present-day Balamumu immigrant, married uxorilocally, has brought his mainland totems with him. But whether they will become adopted more widely or not depends upon his influence. If a man has numerous followers – either by marrying many wives and producing many children, or by exerting himself as a community leader – e.g. as a ritual specialist, an active figure in the settlement of disputes, etc.– his totems may 'take on'. People wish to identify with him. There is thus an important personal element in totemic innovation. This also takes the form of innovation via aesthetic creation. One single man has personally produced more new 'totemic' songs than the rest of the tribe put together, including new songs relating to military forces on Groote Eylandt in World War II ('Army'), a song about 'Airbase', and a song about 'Catalina' flying boats. He *likes* singing, and though he belongs to a clan with only one other adult married male member, he has contributed vastly and disproportionately to the totemic repertoire of the Groote Eylandters. This gives us an important clue: the myth and song are the essential ingredients of the totemic system. *Alauwudawara* means totem, song, myth, story, work of art, painting, string figure, and even small objects that the aborigines find attractive or intriguing: a mole on the body, or a little medical phial. Totems exist, then, primarily in a mythological context, not a logical context, let alone a sociological one. They develop very largely through the self-development of myth and song, and although items important in a utilitarian sense may well be portrayed in myth and song, this is by no means always the case, as we have seen. Perhaps only an ethnomusicologist steeped in the musical culture of Groote Eylandt could estimate how far the intrinsic *musical* appeal of a particular song is a significant factor in effecting wider social acceptance of a new song, but I do not think this should be forgotten – 'Army', 'Airbase', and 'Catalina' were greatly enjoyed, and, moreover, had the attraction of novelty (though 'written' in quite traditional style).

But songs are not created by culture-free men: the innovatory songman belongs to a particular clan. His song is therefore his clan's song. But the totems do *not* neatly discriminate one clan from another. Since all clans in a moiety share each other's songs and dances, and co-operate in ritual, totems are also shared (Elkin, 1933, p. 121). There are no 'diacritical' subsidiary totems discriminating clans bearing the Central Hill totemic myth complex from each other; but of the clans sharing Ship in common, one clan has the further totems Conch Shell and Bailer Shell; another, the further totem, Coconut; another, the Catalina set, plus Dove and Turtle; and the fourth (on Woodah Island, near Balamumu territory) no further totems other than mainland ones (this clan is even reported, wrongly, in the literature, as being a Balamumu, not a Wanindiljaugwa, clan).

Among the Wanindiljaugwa, the clan, in fact, is largely significant only at the ritual level, though, in the light of the advanced breakdown of Groote Eylandt religion, I cannot speak too confidently here. Otherwise its functions seem singularly limited; the moiety is far more important, notably in regulating marriage, and even, to a great extent, in ritual (cf. the parallel Dua and Jiridja moiety ritual divisions on the mainland). It is probably for this reason that the 'diacritical' competences of totemism remain unfulfilled on Groote Eylandt; totems are shared and borrowed, and the exact status of minor totems is unclear, even whether they are to be regarded as totems at all. Some people recognize more totems than others (hence minor discrepancies – omissions or additions – in my two lists in the different articles cited above).

For many clans, there is no 'main' totem. For others, people normally refer to one particular totem first, e.g. the Southeast wind for the Wanindiljaugwa clan, though they do not conceptualize or verbalize this as any kind of 'principal' or 'main' totem. (But since they have no word for 'clan', 'moiety', or 'tribe', either, this linguistic evidence is not conclusive.)

The allocation of totems to particular social groups is not, therefore, an intellectual attempt to order the universe according to some assumed immanent logic visible in Nature itself. The social framework of clan and moiety is the matrix within which totems are distributed. The social order structures the totemic distribution. But totems rise (and probably fall) in unpredictable ways: men immigrate, create songs, assert leadership. (In genealogies, a handful only of the 'great men' of two, rarely three, generations ago, actually remembered by living men, are recorded. Further back than that, no genealogical extensions or connections exist.)

The appearance of compendious systematization can be 'substantiated' only by selective and unscientific concentration upon the more systematic parts of the totemic compendium to the exclusion of all the contingent parts I have touched upon. I have therefore tried to avoid speaking of a 'totemic system', but rather of a 'collection', for the process by which the totemic compendium develops is not via a logical ordering of the aborigines' world according to binary or any other discriminations (though this may be an *element*, e.g. the Southeast/Northwest wind division, empirically large or small according to the culture in question): the totemic 'collection' accretes, cumulates, forms agglomerations of items unconnected in systematic logic or in Nature, according to a variety of principles of association. Instead, therefore, of conceiving of the totemic schema as an ordered totality, I have called it 'agglomerative, arbitrary, and fortuitous'. Even such large totemic compendia as that of the Aranda and Loritja (containing 442 recorded 'totems') seems to be still of the same type, and not more 'systematic', despite the abundance of items represented (Spencer & Gillen, 1904, Appendix B, pp. 767-773).

As far as the validation of behaviours is concerned, we find only very limited segments of aboriginal cultures expressly 'covered' in totemic mythology: man *v.* animals, and aborigines *v.* Makassarese. The 'explanation' of major topographical features is slightly more exhaustive of the major features, and therefore more satisfactory to those who expect to find system (though, for example, there is no myth to account for the separate existence of Bickerton Island, or Woodah, Chasm, Winchelsea, and other islands, or for Groote's relationship to the mainland).

These radical differences in principle of association must not be obscured. They are well expressed as an analytical distinction in a quite different substantive area, in Vygotsky's scientific dialogue with Piaget on the language and thought of the child (1962).

Vygotsky distinguishes, first, as a phase-type in the development of childhood thinking, the *unorganized congeries* or 'heap' where:

'The heap, consisting of disparate objects grouped together without any basis reveals a diffuse undirected extension of the meaning of the sign (artificial word) to inherently unrelated objects linked by chance in the child's perception.

At that stage, word meaning denotes nothing more to the child than a *vague syncretic conglomeration of individual objects* that have somehow or other coalesced into an image in his mind' (pp. 59-60).

The only order provided here, connecting the objects linked together in reality as well as in the child's mind, is the order provided by social cadres – just as the clans provide a framework for the ordering of totems.

Congeries are sharply distinguished from *complexes*, where:

'In a complex, individual objects are united in the child's mind not only by his subjective impressions but also by *bonds actually existing between these objects. . . .* In a complex, the bonds between its components are *concrete and factual* rather than abstract and logical . . .' (p. 61).

Finally, both congeries and complexes (within both of which classes he distinguishes sub-classes) are distinguished from *concepts*:

'Since a complex is not formed on the plane of abstract logical thinking, the bonds that create it, as well as the bonds it helps to create, lack logical unity; they may be of many different kinds. *Any factually present* connection may lead to the inclusion of a given element into a complex. That is the main difference between a complex and a concept. While a concept groups objects according to one attribute, the bonds relating the elements of a complex to the whole and to one another may be as diverse as the contacts and relationships of the elements are in reality' (p. 62).

'The advanced concept presupposes more than unification. To form such a concept it is necessary to *abstract*, to *single out* elements, and to view the abstracted elements apart from the totality of concrete experience in which they are embedded. In genuine concept formation, it is equally important to unite and to separate: synthesis must be combined with analysis.

Complex thinking cannot do both. Its very essence is over-
abundance, overproduction of connections, and weakness in
abstraction' (p. 76).

'. . . A concept emerges only when the abstracted traits are
synthesized anew and the resulting abstract synthesis
becomes the main instrument of thought' (p. 78).

Which brings us back to Evans-Pritchard. The totemic
distribution we have examined is founded either upon 'congeries
thinking' or 'complex thinking', not upon 'thinking in concepts'.
I am not saying that the aborigines are incapable of thinking
conceptually, however. Indeed, they exhibit no mean capacity
in this direction when we examine a quite separate ordering of
the natural environment which they have developed, independently of the totemic 'ordering', that is, in their ethnobotanical
and ethnozoological schemas. Elsewhere (Worsley, 1961,
pp. 153-190) I have listed the hundreds of species of plants and
animals which the aborigines not merely know of, but also
classify broadly together into such taxa as *jinungwangba* (large
land-animals), *wuradjidja* (flying things, including birds),
augwalja (fish and other sea-animals), etc. – and which they
also cross-associated (complex-wise) into ecologically interconnected elements. It is for this reason, no doubt, that
Donald Thomson (trained as a natural scientist) described a
similar ethnobotanical-zoological system of the Wik-Monkan of
Northern Queensland as having 'some resemblance to a simple
Linnaean classification' (Thomson, 1946, p. 167).

It is only *proto*-Linnaean not merely because the aborigines
fail to develop any more adequate criteria of classification than
rather gross, and largely external, indicators such as shape,
size, habitat, etc., but because they limit their inspection to
species of utilitarian value, for the most part (here, in the
secular order, utilitarian selection *is* important, whereas in the
totemic ordering it is not crucial). They have a social interest,
particularly, in edible species of animal, which are more finely
discriminated than non-edible or non-usable species. (Leach
(1964) has recently applied this insight, in a much more
extended way, in a fascinating analysis of animal categories
embedded in ordinary English speech.)

Peter Worsley

Granted this social motivation and selection (and, thereby, the absence of 'useless' species in the system, which a more value-free scientific classification would necessarily entail), the classification thereafter proceeds along proto-scientific lines. But this system of classification is not only a parallel, and quite separate, system from the totemic compendium; it is organized on quite different principles, and involves conceptual thinking, not thinking primarily in congeries or complexes. So we have two systems of classification, not one, and it is illegitimate to conceive of the totemic distribution as representing the only (let alone the major) way in which cultural ordering of the environment is achieved by the aborigines, let alone to construct (or assume) a unitary, overall, master synthesis, or to assume that Order I = Order II.

We have, in fact, discerned three separable areas:

1. The totemic elements themselves, which are congeries-like in that the associations between totems are of mythological derivation, and are therefore random, fortuitous, or haphazard (unless we start making assumptions about subconscious levels of association), though established along quite discernible, multiple lines of association (connections in Nature, connections in myth, connections effected in historical cultural experience, etc.).
2. The order introduced into this totemic collection from without, i.e. the framework provided by the association of totem and clan/moiety.
3. The proto-scientific classification.

Like Burridge, rather than assume that the totemic logic reposes upon universal traits of human thought, we have examined Groote Eylandt totemism within the context of a specific cultural idiom, and particularly 'within the context of a corpus of myths'. As he remarks, 'the approach suggested emphasizes content, regarding form as simply a convenient if revealing mode of ordering the content in a particular cultural context'. This, we should emphasize, is not mere empiricism, since it is itself a mode of analysis that traces the principles of totemic association and does not merely describe (cf. *supra*, pp. 94, 109, 111-112).

154

Lévi-Strauss, Burridge remarks, 'goes to form rather than content', producing a 'spurious uniformity'. He tends to assume an overall closeness of fit between classificatory systems within the same culture and the framework of the social order that simply is not necessarily always, or often, the case. What he sometimes produces, therefore, is the anthropological equivalent of formalism in sociology, explicitly so in his formulation of totemism as

'. . . an original logic, a direct expression of the structure of the mind (and behind the mind, probably, of the brain), . . . not an inert product of the action of the environment on an amorphous consciousness' (Lévi-Strauss, 1962a, p. 130; 1964a, p. 90).[4]

This logic, he says, is built into 'the laws of language and even of thought'.

The Australians, are indeed victims of order, what Lévi-Strauss himself refers to as the 'ravages' of 'l'esprit de système'. Of course, the 'laws of language' might seriously mislead us, if, without going to Australia, we tried to erect a logical scheme which seriously attributed some inner conceptual and social meaning to the French classification of all things into masculine and feminine. A similar Procrustean tendency to that which appears in this treatment of totemism is visible in the treatment of Australian marriage, which has long been dealt with as if the reality coincided with the ideology expressed in the form of an algebraically representable set of rules, yielding a marriage system in which there is overall interlocking consistency, arising from a neat and rational exchange of women. In fact, the analytical problem lies in the reconciliation of prescriptive marriage rules with the normal condition of massive divergence from these rules: the problem of delineating the principles according to which the re-ordering of relationships is effect. Here, the major breakthrough has been Hart and Pilling's study of the Tiwi (1961),[5] where marriage is set within the context of struggles for power and status. What one might call 'political adultery' throws out any possibility of overall system, since women change hands faster than they do in Hollywood.

There *is* no overall order, only areas of consistency inconsistently linked together, on the basis of the structural primacy of the two basic groups originally, and correctly, highlighted by Radcliffe-Brown (1931): the nuclear family and the sibling group.

Aboriginal marriage is not an internally consistent system of self-reciprocating equilibrium. Mechanical analogies, as usual, are of dubious value for the study of human cultural activity, since deviation and manipulation are omnipresent, both because people have differential interests and because they innovate.

As a further instance of the overstructuring in the analysis of Australian society, Hiatt has demonstrated how the close nomadic association between the patrilineal horde and its local territory, postulated by Radcliffe-Brown, just is not the case (Hiatt, 1962).

'Only disconnect' would surely be sage advice to the systematizer faced with the temptations of Australia.

Totemism is, of course, not merely a cognitive ordering, it also has affectual and evaluative meaning. Totemism, in fact, to the aborigine, expresses symbolically the totality of his society and its relationship to the wider order of Nature and the supernatural. It also has institutional implications. It deals with the relatively fixed basic units of clan and moiety, and provides a super-empirical rationale for the order of earthly life. But other classifications, e.g. that involved in the terminological and social ordering of marriage and kinship, deal with much more fluid and manipulable matters. Kinship classification is not just an ordering; it is a set of claims and manipulations (not just – neutrally – 'exchanges'.) So there is a fundamental difference between these two types of classification, and they must be kept analytically distinct. Further, one might observe that there is yet another system of classification – a linguistic one – contained in the Groote Eylandt system of noun classification that is quite unconnected with totemic classification, proto-scientific classification, or any other (and is largely congeries-like rather than conceptual; see Worsley, 1954).

Finally, on binary discrimination. Undoubtedly, as Simmel long ago demonstrated, similarity and difference lend themselves to expression within a two-cell matrix. Indeed, other, more complex multiple combinations are likely to be finally subsumable within such a framework also. Out of dozens of political parties, for example, alliances of government and opposition are formed. The binary form is thus extremely widespread. But it is by no means universal. In some political systems – as in Indonesia today – the several parties just remain several. Indeed, not the binary form, but *unity* is the ultimate residual. There are one-party states, and governments which give representation to *all* parties.

One should, therefore, not be too bemused by the binary fashion. Once upon a time (from Vico to Hegel and beyond) it was triads. Now numerological fashion has changed – binary analysis is illuminating, but if erected into an absolute and universal metaphysic, instead of being used heuristically, it becomes numerology and fashion, not science.

NOTES

1. Again, though I share similar (not the same) misgivings as to the value of Marxist 'laws of dialectics' as a whole to those expressed by Mills (1963, footnotes to pp. 129, 130), in so far as there might conceivably be any 'dialectical principles', they could not be 'dialectics of Nature', *pace* Engels, or even 'in Nature'; dialectics are of the mind (which is itself, to be sure, 'in' Nature).
2. Durkheim was therefore wrong to insist that social facts are *things*; apart from their being abstractions from *process*, they are also not 'thing-like' in being exterior, as Durkheim insisted, but have to be subjectively 'understood' as Weber showed (Durkheim, 1950). They are all mediated via consciousness, and are evaluated. They are not likely even to be perceived at all unless they have 'social value', to use Radcliffe-Brown's term.
3. It is purely an empirical matter whether such closeness exists or not. As a parallel, Macbeath (1952) shows how legal and moral codes, in some societies, are closely sustained by religious validations, and are 'legitimated', or derive their rationale, by reference to beliefs about the supernatural. Other societies, however, do not connect legal, moral, or 'jural' systems closely to the religious system. It is interesting that Nadel (1954), who studied the religion of a society where religious beliefs and practices only very slightly obtruded into everyday life, is careful to talk about the 'competences' and not the 'functions' of religion. Potentially religion *can*, say, provide a rationale for a work ethic; this is – in the permissive mode of speech – possible, even likely or common. But not always; so 'function' has too many deterministic and universalistic overtones, too many biological-organic holistic associations, to satisfy.
4. Cf. Lévi-Strauss (1963a), p. 65: 'Time and space modalities of the universal laws which make up the unconscious activity of the mind'.
5. Cf. David Lockwood's critique of another 'powerless' reciprocity-model, that of Talcott Parsons, in Lockwood (1956).

REFERENCES

BERGSON, H. 1958 (88th edn.). *Les Deux Sources de la morale et de la religion*. Paris: Bibliothèque de Philosophie Contemporaine.

DURKHEIM, E. 1950 (8th edn.). *Rules of Sociological Method*. Glencoe, Ill.: The Free Press.

—— 1957. *The Elementary Forms of the Religious Life*. London: Allen & Unwin.

ELKIN, A. P. 1933. *Studies in Australian Totemism*. Sydney: Australian National Research Council. Oceania Monographs No. 2.

EVANS-PRITCHARD, E. E. 1934. Lévy-Bruhl's Theory of Primitive Mentality (extract from the *Bulletin of the Faculty of Arts* **2**, part I). Cairo: Imprimerie de l'Institut Français d'Archéologie Orientale.

FORTES, M. 1945. *The Dynamics of Clanship among the Tallensi*. London: Oxford University Press (International African Institute).

HART, C. W. M. & PILLING, A. R. 1961. *The Tiwi of North Australia*. New York: Holt, Rinehart & Wilson.

HIATT, L. R. 1962. Local Organization among the Australian Aborigines. *Oceania* **32**: 267-286.

LEACH, E. R. 1964. Anthropological Aspects of Language: Animal Categories and Verbal Abuse. In Eric H. Lenneberg (ed.), *New Directions in the Study of Language*. Cambridge, Mass.: M.I.T. Press, pp. 23-63.

LÉVI-STRAUSS, C. 1962a. *Le Totémisme aujourd'hui*. Paris: Presses Universitaires de France (English translation, 1964a. *Totemism*. London: Merlin Press).

—— 1962b. *La Pensée sauvage*. Paris: Plon.

—— 1963a. *Structural Anthropology*. New York: Basic Books.

LOCKWOOD, D. 1956. Some Remarks on *The Social System*. *British Journal of Sociology* **7**: 134-146.

MACBEATH, A. 1952. *Experiments in Living*. London: Macmillan.

MILLER, HENRY. 1936. *Black Spring*. Paris: Obelisk Press.

MILLS, C. WRIGHT. 1963. *The Marxists*. Harmondsworth: Pelican Books.

NADEL, S. F. 1954. *Nupe Religion*. London: Routledge & Kegan Paul.

RADCLIFFE-BROWN, A. R. 1931. *The Social Organization of Australian Tribes*. Melbourne: Macmillan.

SPENCER, B. & GILLEN, F. J. 1904. *The Northern Tribes of Central Australia*. London: Macmillan.

THOMSON, D. F. 1946. Names and Naming in the Wik Monkan Tribe. *Journal of the Royal Anthropological Institute* **76**, Part II: 157-167.

WORSLEY, P. 1954. Noun-Classification in Australian & Bantu: Formal or Semantic? *Oceania* **24**: 275-288.

—— 1955. Totemism in a Changing Society. *American Anthropologist* **57**: 851-861.

—— 1956. Emile Durkheim's Theory of Knowledge. *Sociological Review* **4**: 47-62.

—— 1961. The Utilization of Food Resources by an Australian Aboriginal Tribe. *Acta Ethnographica* **10**: 153-190. Budapest: Academiae Scientiarum Hungaricae.

VYGOTSKY, L. S. 1962. *Thought and Language* (edited and translated by E. Hanfmann & G. Vankar). (Studies in Communication.) Cambridge, Mass.: M.I.T. Press.

Robin Fox

Totem and Taboo Reconsidered

It is appropriate that a symposium devoted to totemism and myth should consider Freud's *Totem and Taboo*.[1] This book is about totemism, and uses, in one of its most important conclusions, the language of myth. Anthropologists have dismissed it as mythology masquerading as science. Freud himself ruefully commented that Kroeber had put it into the category of a 'Just-So Story'.[2] But Kroeber, in his second thoughts on the book, did try to interpret the myth – to tell us what it *really* meant.[3] We ourselves have been discussing what myths really mean and what totemism really means, so perhaps we can treat sympathetically Freud's myth of totemism and look for the possible eternal truths that underlie the graphic description of the controversial 'event'.

Both Freud and Lévi-Strauss are basically interested in the same question: how did *Homo* come to be *sapiens*? What sets man off from Nature while leaving him part of Nature? For Freud, this is a result of the imposition of restraints on free sexual activity as a result of strong feelings – guilt, fear, fraternity, obedience, incest, etc. For Lévi-Strauss (1949), in his earlier work, it is a result not of negative injunctions but of the positive value of exchange, i.e. of women. In his later work (e.g. Lévi-Strauss, 1962a, 1962b) the distinguishing feature of man is also exchange, but exchange of information rather than women. 'Articulate thought' and its basic processes are at the back of what is characteristically human. Even human society is simply a working-out in institutional form of these basic thought processes. 'Totemism' for Freud sets man over against Nature because it involves a constraint of 'natural activity'. For Lévi-Strauss it also sets man over against Nature because it involves the *use* of Nature for social classification. Thus for Freud the breakthrough is an affective phenomenon; for Lévi-Strauss it is intellectual. A good deal of what Lévi-Strauss regards as basic, Freud would no doubt have dismissed as

161

rationalization. Most of what Freud regards as basic, Lévi-Strauss would dismiss as a failure to be truly human (Lévi-Strauss, 1962a, p. 103; 1964a, p. 71). Yet both are psychological reductionists. Freud reduces to the power of the instinctual processes, and Lévi-Strauss to the power of logical processes. For Freud the world of Nature is something onto which man can project his emotions: for Lévi-Strauss it is a source of metaphors for social thinking. For Freud 'totemism' involves a relation between human needs and emotions and the world of Nature: for Lévi-Strauss it involves a relation between human thought-processes and the natural world.

Over against both these positions I suppose we must set the 'sociological' position which sees man's distinctive characteristic as 'society' with its norms, rules, and customs. This stems from Durkheim, who, like Freud, went to the Australian aborigines for his data and inspiration. Lévi-Strauss, although in the general Durkheimian tradition, rejects his views on totemism and religion because they reduce it, in the last analysis, to a sentimental basis (Lévi-Strauss, 1962a, p. 102; 1964a, p. 71). The rejection would also apply to Radcliffe-Brown – interpreter of Durkheim to social anthropology – and his theory of sentiment and ritual. Thus, although man is clearly an emotive, cognitive, and social animal, opinion differs as to which of these aspects is basic and explanatory. In this essay we shall be concerned with the potential explanatory value of Freud's approach in *Totem and Taboo*.

Freud, taking his cue from contemporary anthropology, linked totemism firmly with exogamy – or rather with incest taboos – and his concern with totemism is incidental to his concern with incest. Totemism, as a system of exogamous clans, is interesting in so far as it is an extreme example of the renunciation of women for sexual purposes. Speaking of the arrangement of phratries (moieties), sub-phratries, and totem clans, he says, 'The result (and therefore the purpose) of these arrangements cannot be doubted: they bring about a still further restriction on the choice of marriage and on sexual liberty' (Freud, 1950, p. 8). He saw in the Australians an extreme example of incest and exogamy restrictions, and he saw these as linked to groups whose characteristic was a myth of descent from, and a 'ritual attitude' towards, some natural species. The 'ritual attitude' was that of 'taboo' which he saw as a case of emotional ambivalence – love-hate – towards the tabooed object. The attitude was characteristic of certain types of neurosis, and its direction towards animals was found in children, as was the expression of cannibalistic wishes and the associated guilt. Freud brilliantly pulls these strands together to explain, via the myth of the primal horde, the origins of totemistic observances, exogamy, incest horror – and incidentally religion and civilization. At some point, he is saying, the breakthrough from superior primate to *Homo sapiens* must have occurred; somehow, man became an exogamous animal, and this is how it 'must have' happened. What is more, *Homo sapiens* cannot forget it. We persistently re-affirm our implication in that original deed which made us men.

Freud treats all the elements of the 'totemic' complex as part of a single 'original' pattern exhibited today only in the culture of the most primitive of men – the Australian aborigines. Thus prohibitions on incest, rules of exogamy, unilineal descent, totemic classification, the ritual attitude to the totem animal, the food taboos ceremonially broken, and all the paraphernalia of Australian totemism were seen as *necessarily* connected, and the myth made the connection as a myth should do. But if we raise our sights a little from Australia then the necessity of the connection becomes less obvious and the myth less plausible. Goldenweiser was the first to clear up this point. The two essential features – on the one hand, the system of totemic classification, and, on the other, the ritual attitude to the totem – do not seem to be necessarily connected and neither seems to be necessarily connected with unilineal descent. Certainly the taboo-killing-eating-guilt complex of the Australians seems to be unique. Freud's answer to this problem is implicitly evolutionary. These things were necessarily associated in the beginning and have been preserved in the primitive aborigines. Other cultures have lost them or transmuted them, without losing the basic motivations that brought them into being. Thus we still renounce sisters and kill fathers in various guises and feel guilty about the whole thing, but we no longer – except as children – project this onto the animal kingdom. To this kind of thinking we have long since returned the verdict of 'not proven'. But this does not mean not plausible or not enlightening. I shall argue, not that the myth is untrue, for such a criterion is not really applicable to myths, but that it is not plausible – it does not resolve enough of the problems that it seeks to cover. To do this I shall look at some criticisms both implied and overt, of *Totem and Taboo*, and try to assess what Freud really meant. Then I will discuss the implications of my interpretation for an understanding of some of the totem complex.

Let us look first at some recent writings on a similar theme, which seem at first sight to run counter to the Freudian position on incest. Goody (1956), writing of incest and adultery, points out that we have to treat unilineal societies differently from bilateral when trying to explain the incidence and severity of restrictions on heterosexual activity. There is, he says, a 'bilateral bias' in incest theories which have been developed to fit our own peculiar system of kinship in which the nuclear family is the key unit. In his division of types of theory, he puts Freud along with Malinowski, Radcliffe-Brown, Seligman, Murdock, and Parsons, into the 'internal-relations-of-the-family' box. In contradistinction to these, Goody argues that in unilineal societies, the incest/exogamy prohibitions 'cut across' the family in different ways. Matrilineal societies are more concerned with the mother and sister categories than with the daughter category, because the mother and sister are members of the descent group whereas the daughter is not. Patrilineal societies are not so much concerned with the descent-group females as with the wives of members of the group. This is related to (*a*) the fact that in matrilineal societies the mothers and sisters, and in patrilineal societies the wives, are the progenitrices of the lineages, and (*b*) the solidarity of the males of the descent group, although this is rather an implicit argument. For some reason or other, then, the males of the group must not 'interfere with the sexuality of' the women who reproduce it. This saves the mother on both counts. She is, in matrilineal societies, a senior clanswoman, and, in patrilineal, a senior wife. Note in passing that Goody agrees with Mrs Seligman (1950) in regarding generation and seniority as important factors along with lineality, especially where the potential offender is a junior male.

Now, Leach (1961) too has recently been arguing, in opposition to Fortes who still seems to hold with the universality of intrafamilial incest taboos, that these restrictions fall differently in different unilineal systems. I do not know, but I imagine that Leach would, like Goody, link Freud to Fortes and set both over against his own position which in fact parallels Goody's. Leach seems to be saying that for some patrilineal societies at least, a man's mother is his affine. He presents evidence to show that some patrilineal peoples treat intercourse with her as adultery, which ties up with Goody's notion of her as a senior wife of the lineage. It follows that in matrilineal societies, a man's daughter is in a similar position. She is not a member of his descent group and restrictions, if any, on their intercourse are not the equivalent of restrictions on consanguineously related persons. From the point of view of the junior generation, we see that in some matrilineal societies, then, a girl's father is an affinal relative.

Putting these two contemporary views together we reach the following conclusions:

(a) Freud represents an 'internal-relations-of-the-family' position as regards the determinants of restrictions on intrafamilial intercourse;

(b) this is inadequate when dealing with unilineal societies where the incidence of such restrictions differs according to the principles of descent employed. In matrilineal societies the daughter, and in patrilineal the mother, while possibly coming under some ban, do not come under the ban on intralineage sexuality;

(c) that generation and authority, and the solidarity of the lineage males are important contributory factors.

Let us look at the naïve, psychological-mythological arguments of *Totem and Taboo* in the light of these essentially sociological conclusions. The first point to notice is that, in dealing with the Australians, Freud was in fact dealing with unilineal societies. If Goody and Leach are right in their analysis of these societies, and if Freud does indeed represent an 'internal-relations-of-the-family' position, then we can only conclude that in his greatest work on incest he missed the point. However, when discussing the 'remarkable' prohibition – that people of the same totem may not have sexual relations with each other – he says:

'Since totems are hereditary and not changed by marriage, it is easy to follow the consequences of the prohibition. Where, for instance, descent is through the female line, if a man of the Kangaroo totem marries a woman of the Emu totem, all the children, both boys and girls, belong to the Emu clan. The totem regulation will therefore make it impossible for a son of this marriage to have incestuous intercourse with his mother or sisters, who are Emus like himself' (Freud, 1950, p. 5).

He then adds this footnote:

'On the other hand, at all events, so far as this prohibition is concerned, the father, who is a Kangaroo, is free to commit incest with his daughters, who are Emus. If the totem descended through the *male* line, however, the Kangaroo father would be prohibited from intercourse with his daughters (since all his children would be Kangaroos), whereas the son would be free to commit incest with his mother. These implications of the totem prohibitions suggest that descent through the female line is older than that through the male, since there are grounds for thinking that the totem prohibitions were principally directed against the incestuous desires of the son.'

Now it is clear from this passage that Freud is quite well aware of the precise differential effects of unilineal descent on incest prohibitions. The prohibitions fall quite differently across the 'family' in each case. He sees the prohibitions as properties of the totem clan, not the family, and the 'implications' of this are that the full range of prohibitions is possible only when both types of descent are present. He clinches this in the following:

'We can see then, that these savages have an unusually great horror of incest, or are sensitive on the subject to an unusual degree, and that they combine this with a peculiarity which remains obscure to us of replacing real blood-relationships by totem-kinship. This latter contrast must not, however, be too much exaggerated, and we must remember that *the totem prohibitions include those against real incest as a special case'* (Freud, 1950, p. 6) (my italics).

Thus 'real' blood relationship is seen as occurring only in the totem clan, and the familial prohibitions are a *special case* of totem prohibitions. This is pure Goody-Leach in argument. But Freud goes further. He tries to establish a primacy in time between the two types of descent. Matrilineal comes first and patrilineal comes later and 'sticks' as it were. (Note also that fraternal solidarity figures prominently in Freud's argument. The sons of the primal horde learn it in exile after being driven out by the father, and it weighs heavily in their decision to renounce the women of the horde (Freud, 1950, p. 14).)

I will develop this point about the chronological priority of matrilineality later, but in the meantime we must clear away some of the most famous anthropological criticisms of *Totem and Taboo*: those made by Kroeber. We must do this because, having established Freud as essentially holding a descent theory of prohibitions in this book, we must rebut Kroeber's charge that he was really talking about recurrent Oedipal situations, that is, that he held an 'internal-relations-of-the-family' theory. Ernest Jones has said that Kroeber's criticisms comprise not refutation but merely disbelief, and there is something in this view (Jones, 1957, p. 335). Kroeber's second thoughts on the subject were, however, more charitable than his first. While still dismissing as fantastic the 'historical' claims of the myth of the primal horde, he is willing to allow that it has some value as a 'timeless' psychological interpretation. Freud's 'ambiguity' on this issue 'leads him to state a timeless psychological explanation as if it were a historical one. . . . His argument is evidently ambiguous as between historical thinking and psychological thinking.' The clue to this Kroeber finds in Freud's statement that the great 'event' was to be construed as 'typical'. 'A typical event', says Kroeber, 'historically speaking, is a recurrent one. This can hardly be admitted for the father-slaying, eating and guilt sense.' Thus we are only left with the 'concept of the psychologically potential. . . . Certain psychic processes tend always to be operative and to find expression in human institutions.' These are the processes associated with the Oedipal situation which are summed up in the myth.

Now what are we to make of this reasoning? Does Freud indeed state the argument ambiguously? This is not how it strikes me. It seems quite plain from *Totem and Taboo* that the *event* which Freud refers to was in fact an historical event. If it was typical it was typical of a certain stage of human development, and if recurrent it was recurrent in the sense which Freud makes quite clear, that is, that it happened more than once during this stage. Had Freud stated his conclusions in the language of evolutionary anthropology instead of in the language of myth, Kroeber might have got the point. What Freud is saying is that during a certain stage of human social evolution – the stage when the higher anthropoids lived in hordes of the kind described by Atkinson and Darwin – the event to which he refers occurred over and over again in horde after horde. Freud clearly does not wish to state a timeless psychological truth in mythological form. His myth is an *origin* myth and unambiguously so. He is concerned with the 'breakthrough from nature to culture' (Lévi-Strauss, 1949, p. 31), which happened during a particular historical period. This 'event' was the most important in the history of man – it was what made him man – and because of this it continues to leave its mark.

Now Kroeber may very well be correct in saying that the circumstances described in the myth are constantly renewed. With the socialization of each infant – the domestication of each little anthropoid – the breakthrough has to be achieved once more. It may also be true that Freud's myth describes the processes involved in this socialization. But this is Kroeber's theory, not Freud's, and what I am arguing is that in *Totem and Taboo* it is not the function of the myth to describe these recurrent processes. Freud is not concerned here with recurrent psychic events, but with the *transmission* of motives down the generations. These motives were learned once and for all at a certain stage of human evolution. To fit Kroeber's interpretation the theory would have to pertain to the 'family', generation by generation, and its Oedipal processes. But Freud, as we have seen, is quite explicit that the taboos are a feature of the totem *clan* in which they are inherited. In other words, to borrow a structuralist phrase, they are a 'descent phenomenon'. And this is the rub. The taboos and phobias are not 'generated' in the 'family' and then 'extended' as Murdock (1949, p. 291) puts it, they were generated in the primal event and henceforth *inherited* in the totem clan. 'Family' incest is a 'special case' of clan incest. The full range of taboos within the family is a function of double descent, a juxtaposition of matrilineally and later patrilineally inherited taboos. This makes nonsense of Kroeber's 'ambiguity' accusation and his reinterpretation, which utterly destroys Freud's meaning. Freud presses on to argue that, the taboos being inherited, they must have had an origin in time, and as the clans claim descent from animals whom they identify with the original ancestor, and as they inherit certain 'ritual attitudes' – including the taboo-killing-eating complex – it seems reasonable to examine the rituals as a clue to the origin.

What ambiguity there is lies in the nature of this 'inheritance'. Freud shrugs this one off. It obviously takes place, so the mechanisms of it can be taken as given (Freud, 1950, p. 157). It may be a Lamarckian inheritance or it may be via learning. Here the Kroeberian and Freudian theories have a meeting-point. If the inheritance is cultural, then a certain set of recurring phenomena may be necessary for the learning to take place. Freud may well have welcomed this suggestion, but it would have been a supplement to his historical analysis, not a substitute for it. Freud's theory does not require the family, nor does it require the Oedipal situation to keep recurring. It only requires the historical event to have taken place and its results to have been inherited.

Thus we have established (*a*) that Freud did not regard incest motivations as the outcome of recurrent psychic events within the family, but as inherited characteristics acquired in a traumatic way during the horde stage of social evolution; and (*b*) that, far from having a bilateral or familial bias as regards incest theories, he saw that for the Australians the factor of unilineal descent was crucially related to the incidence of prohibitions. But what is strongly implied in his whole argument is something that goes beyond a recognition of the *effects* of unilineality. It is a recognition that motivations and prohibitions are an integral part of unilineality. It is not that we have such-and-such taboos and phobias because we are matrilineal, but that we are matrilineal because we have such-and-such taboos and phobias.

Now, Freud recognized, as we have seen, that different types of phobia and taboo went with different types of descent system. But his view required him to take neither the feelings nor the institutions for granted, but to seek for the interaction between them. Thus we have to look at the other side of the coin presented by Goody and Leach and ask what are the motivations that prompt matrilineal and patrilineal peoples to deny procreative powers to fathers and mothers respectively. The affect surrounding these denials suggests that something more than the slavish following of custom is involved. These denials are not made simply to accommodate the logic of the descent system but because they are deeply felt. If the people did not feel moved to make them, then the system would not be what it is.

Let us then set on one side Freud's phylogenetic questions for the moment and instead of seeing the myth of the primal horde as a myth of the origins of everything, see it simply as a myth of the origins of matrilineal systems – for on Freud's logic these should be the outcome of the great event. Freud's remark that 'there are grounds for thinking that totem prohibitions were principally directed against the incestuous desires of the son' clearly refers to the situation in the primal horde where the dominant father drove out the sons whose desires were directed against their sisters and mothers. Having rebelled and killed the father (and eaten him), the sons were then in a position to take over their mothers and sisters, but they did not do so. Remorse over their terrible deed and 'deferred obedience' to the father led them to renounce these women. Guilt about their deed led them to project their father feelings on to the totem animal in the form of an eating taboo, and fraternal solidarity led them to the ceremonial breaking of the taboo. The exogamous totemic groups we are left with then, are matrilineages – brothers, sisters, and mothers.

Let us look, then, at an ideal-type matrilineal situation. Here a striking fact emerges at once, namely, the elimination of the father. I do not need to elaborate this to an audience of anthropologists in terms of the structural non-necessity of the father/husband role. Schneider (1961) has put this succinctly into a few elegant formulations. But along with this elimination of the father goes the renunciation of the women. However, although the women are renounced their children are not. The brothers claim the children of the women as their own – even to the extent of denying the physiological role of the father in their creation. They refuse to believe that the sister's husband can be the creator (father) of *their* children. This constitutes a further elimination of fatherhood – both structurally and physiologically it is denied. It also constitutes the ultimate realization of the incestuous desires of the brothers, realised, it is true, only in fantasy. They cannot have intercourse with their sisters, but they can claim the fruits of their sisters' intercourse and deny the father a role in this process as they deny him a place in the social structure.

If this seems fantastic, then Malinowski's description of Trobriand culture must be fantastic, because this is just what he describes. The Trobrianders are the father-eliminators *par excellence*. They deny the husband/father, through the *urigubu* payment, even the right to support his wife, and their incestuous wishes are evident in myth, dream, and behaviour.[4]

The Trobrianders, however, lack two things essential to Freud's myth: elaborate totem rituals, and remorse and guilt with respect to a symbolic father. As we have seen, not all matrilineal societies are totemic, and this raises a problem. In the Trobriand Islands there is no totem ritual and collective affirmation of solidarity by the brothers. And, indeed, as Fortes (1963) has pointed out, in many matrilineal societies the father is given some part to play in the social system, even if it is only residual or complementary.

Thus Freud's myth can handle totemic matrilineal societies

171

but falls down on the non-totemic. To cover the latter, the myth will have to be modified so that it accounts for matrilineality and the incest wishes but omits the father-slaying and remorse. I suggest the following version:

'In the beginning the sons were kept from the women of the horde by the fathers, and much as they would have liked to, the sons did not kill the fathers but simply withdrew from sexual competition with them. The frustration of their sexual drives was intense enough to be frightening, so much so that when the fathers died (or were maybe driven out) the sons could not face sexuality with the women.[5] Their sexual interest in them was however still intense, so while they took other people's sisters to bed, they acted out the fantasy of having children by their own sisters. They claimed the children as their own and denied the genitor any part in the process. Thus at one stroke they eliminated the fathers both as authorities and as sexual rivals.'

Note that the father is not killed, much less eaten, he is simply defined away. Thus we still have incest wishes and exogamic matrilineal groups, but because no one killed anyone else there is no need for totemism. It is fear of their own motives that leads the brothers to renounce the women, not fear of the dead fathers. We have still not covered all matrilineal societies by any means. Some certainly do not run on the psychic energy provided by sibling incest wishes, but on, for example, a strong mother-child sentiment or some combination of the two (Fox, 1960). But note also that in the above myth we have turned Goody and Leach on their heads. Goody would make incest phobias and anxieties a consequence of matrilineal reckoning; we make them a cause. If they were a consequence, then all matrilineal societies would have them, but they do not. We have allowed for the fact that they are not always a cause. Indeed, the language of cause and effect is misleading here, except in terms of origins. Perhaps we should talk instead of feedback.

We can now complete our re-vamping of the Goody-Leach position by looking at some of the affectual features of patrilineality that it raises to determine whether our method has any success in that direction. Freud did not have a patrilineal origin myth, but it follows that such a myth should be the reverse of the matrilineal. As Leach points out, it should involve the denial of the *mother's* role in the procreation of the child. Interestingly enough, Whiting (n.d.) in a critique of *Totem and Taboo*, proposes an interpretation of the totem myth which suggests just this reversal. He links mother-resentment with sex and weaning in a most ingenious way. Now, the father of the primal horde is a notorious old polygynist, and Whiting links polygyny with the *post-partum sex taboo*. This is the prohibition on intercourse between a man and wife for a period after parturition. Prohibited from intercourse with one wife, he has recourse to others. In the meantime the son is receiving food, stimulation, love, and security from the mother – and these are exclusively his. Sooner or later, though, he has to give way when father comes round again. This return of father, that is, the end of the *post-partum sex taboo*, may or may not coincide with the weaning of the son. If it does, he loses both the exclusive possession of the mother – particularly for sleeping purposes – and the maternal milk with all that this means. If, then, mother turns him out and ceases to feed and stimulate him at the same time, argues Whiting, his resentment will know no bounds. The frustration of his oral drives will lead to cannibalistic-aggressive wishes, directed, of course, towards his mother. Following out the logic of this, Whiting makes the marvellous suggestion, turning Freud on his head, that the totem animal which is ritually slain and eaten is not the father at all but the mother![6] On a cross-cultural survey he finds that totemism linked with food taboos is highly associated with a coincidence of weaning and the end of the *post-partum sex taboo*. Totemism not linked with food taboos is associated with the conditions where suckling carries on but exclusive possession ceases.

This is not the place to go into a full-scale criticism of Whiting's version of the myth. So much rests on his unspecified definition of totemism and on the interpretation of the child's perception of exactly *who* is depriving him of the mother and her food and nurture. Also, to fit my version of Whiting's theory, we need societies which are totemic, patrilineal, and mother-reducing, in the same way that, to fit Freud's myth, we need those which are totemic, matrilineal, and father-denying. Now this does not cover many societies. Not all patrilineal societies have totemic rituals, nor do they all have the extreme mother-denying ideology. For my purposes it suffices to show that situations could exist in which the sons develop extreme resentment against their mothers and so set about reducing the wife/mother role to the point where the mother is denied any part in the procreation of her child. Then we no longer have mothers – only fathers and their sexual partners-cum-incubators. Patrilineal descent can scarcely be avoided in these circumstances.

So much for the elimination of the mother, but there remains, for patrilineal societies, the problem of the renunciation of sisters and daughters. I tend to think, with Goody, that this is not so much renunciation as indifference. The man does not need his sisters to reproduce him as he has not repudiated fatherhood. He can do it himself – with the minimal assistance of his incubator-wife. As the sisters have not really been denied him, in this myth, he has no frustrated desires for them which both attract him towards them and repel him. He may be indifferent to them for a number of reasons, and I have elsewhere (Fox, 1962) tried to show what some of these might be.[7] That none of these are wholly operative can be seen from the fact that a good number of patrilineal societies allow intercourse with the daughter, and, as Goody points out, are not all that troubled by intercourse with the sister. Their chief concern is with the monopoly of the use of the incubator – hence adultery is their main problem. Incest phobias and patrilineal descent seem to be independent variables. Some patrilineal societies are bothered by phobias, others not, and we must look elsewhere than the origins of patrilineal systems for an answer to that problem.

I have dealt here only with unilineal systems, and only with some extreme forms of these. Bilateral systems are very varied, and the motivational, ecological, and adaptational factors involved in their genesis and survival are equally complex. According to Freud's logic, they should come late in the

evolutionary scale. His ladder of kinship evolution would have
to go as follows:

1. Primal hordes
2. Matrilineal hordes
3. Patrilineal descent
4. Fusion of 3 and 4
5. Bilateral systems.

In other words, our system should result from a shedding of
unilineality but a retention of its basic prohibitions as they
affect the 'family'. We have given up the idea of universal social
evolution, and most evidence seems to show extremely simple
groups of hunters and gatherers to be without unilineal
organization, which appears at the 'tribal' level of development.
Matrilineal hordes are a clear impossibility in any case. The
case for a simple evolutionary scale is difficult to sustain.
Kinship systems clearly have diverse origins and are transmuted
from one form to another for a number of reasons. What I have
been suggesting in this paper is that some of these reasons – for
the genesis, change, and persistence of systems – may be
affectual.

I have taken Freud's point (which he held in common with
Goody and Leach) that the incidence of incest taboos is different
in different unilineal systems, and combined this with his
belief that such systems are human inventions with origins in
time and that they are a response to deep feelings about
mothers, sisters, sex, and power. I hope this may have thrown
some light on the nature of unilineal systems by at least
suggesting that the affectual aspects of them are more than just
consequences, and are, in fact, integral parts of the feedback
mechanism that makes the system what it is. What I am *not*
saying is that kinship systems are the products of unconscious
motivations. The convergence of a whole range of factors is
needed to materialize any particular system. What I *am* saying,
quite simply, is that the way people feel about kin is not
necessarily a consequence of the kind of kinship system they
have – it is in fact usually a by-product of the direct learning
of kinship and other norms – and that if they felt differently
then the system would be different. In dealing with static

systems, one can, I suppose, take the feelings as given, but an understanding of them becomes important when one is faced with change.

We have come a long way from Lévi-Strauss's rejection of Freud and Durkheim, and 'totemism' has withered away in the process. Taboo, however, is still with us. This contrasts with Lévi-Strauss, who gets rid of taboo and leaves himself with a rather emasculated totemism. Obviously the approach in this paper is squarely on the side of Freud, Durkheim, and Radcliffe-Brown in the issue of sentiment and social structure. (I share Parsons's (1949) view that Freud and Durkheim were essentially saying the same thing.) The rejection of 'psychology' by structural anthropologists rests on a confusion inherent in Durkheim between sentiment and society, on the one hand, and individual and society, on the other. Also, they have a curious feeling that rules are more stable than emotions. This is patently not so. Rules and customs can be changed overnight – and will be if they fail to meet felt needs – but motives, and especially unconscious motives, are not so readily changeable. It is not, however, a matter of 'reducing' sociological explanations to psychological, but of seeing the relevance of the one for the other. Nor is it a case of declaring for *either* structure *or* sentiment, but of seeing both as part of a single system. This is not an original point, and it has previously been said from within the ranks of British anthropology by S. F. Nadel (1951), but it probably needs saying again. For me, at least, the traditional questions of anthropology cannot be answered by a rigid adherence to one or the other of the emotive, intellectualist, or sociological approaches, for to deny any of these is to deny a part of man's humanity. Nothing human should be alien to the science of man.

NOTES

1. Direct references in this paper are to the Strachey translation published in 1950.
2. Ernest Jones points out that it was in fact R. R. Marrett who made the remark (Jones, 1957, p. 346).
3. Kroeber's first thoughts appeared as 'Totem and Taboo: An Ethnologic Psychoanalysis' in 1920. His second thoughts appeared as 'Totem and Taboo in Retrospect' in 1939.

4. The essential details can be found in Malinowski (1927; 1932). Some passages in Malinowski (1935) are relevant to the contention that it is a denial of physiological paternity that is involved rather than an ignorance of it. This takes us right into the Jones-Malinowski debates concerning the Trobriand Oedipus complex, but, although the argument of this paper is relevant to that controversy, it would involve too long a digression to deal with it here. See, for example, Ernest Jones (1925).

5. For possible responses to frustration, see McClelland (1951, ch. 13).

6. It is curious that the only evidence of cannibalistic wishes that Freud presents in *Totem and Taboo* occurs when discussing the all-important 'return of totemism in childhood' and concerns little Arpad, whose totem phantasies were woven around chickens. His cannibalistic wish was for nothing less than a 'fricassée of mother', on the analogy, Freud ponderously explains, of a fricassée of chicken.

7. I might add here for the record that zoological work seems to indicate that boredom (stimulus saturation) may well be the most important motive for out-breeding among primates.

REFERENCES

FORTES, M. 1963. The Submerged Descent Line in Ashanti. In I. Schapera (ed.), *Studies in Kinship & Marriage*. London: Royal Anthropological Institute.

FOX, J. R. 1960. Therapeutic Rituals and Social Structure in Cochiti Pueblo. *Human Relations* 13: 291-303.

—— 1962. Sibling Incest. *British Journal of Sociology* 13: 128-150.

FREUD, S. 1950. *Totem & Taboo* (authorized translation by James Strachey). London: Hogarth Press.

GOLDENWEISER, A. A. 1910. Totemism: An Analytical Study. *Journal of American Folklore* 23: 179-293. Reprinted with modifications in A. A. Goldenweiser, 1933. *History, Psychology & Culture*. London: Kegan Paul.

GOODY, J. R. 1956. A Comparative Approach to Incest & Adultery. *British Journal of Sociology* 7: 286-305.

JONES, E. 1925. Mother Right & the Sexual Ignorance of Savages. *International Journal of Psycho-Analysis* 6: 109-130.

—— 1957. *Sigmund Freud: Life & Work*. London: Hogarth Press.

KROEBER, A. L. 1920. *Totem & Taboo*: An Ethnologic Psycho-analysis. *American Anthropologist* 22: 48-55.

—— 1939. *Totem & Taboo* in Retrospect. *American Journal of Sociology* 55: 446-451.

LEACH, E. R. 1961. *Rethinking Anthropology*. London: Athlone Press.

LÉVI-STRAUSS, C. 1949. *Les Structures élémentaires de la parenté*. Paris: Presses Universitaires de France.

—— 1962a. *Le Totémisme aujourd'hui*. Paris: Presses Universitaires de France. (English translation, 1964a. *Totemism*. London: Merlin Press.)

LÉVI-STRAUSS, C. 1962b. *La Pensée sauvage*. Paris: Plon.

MALINOWSKI, B. 1927. *Sex & Repression in Savage Society*. London: Kegan & Paul.

—— 1932 (3rd edn.). *The Sexual Life of Savages*. London: Routledge.

—— 1935. *Coral Gardens & Their Magic*. London: Allen & Unwin.

MCCLELLAND, D. C. 1951. *Personality*. New York: Sloane.

MURDOCK, G. P. 1949. *Social Structure*. New York: Macmillan.

NADEL, S. F. 1951. *The Foundations of Social Anthropology*. London: Cohen & West.

PARSONS, T. 1949 (2nd edn.). *The Structure of Social Action: A Study in Social Theory with Special Reference to a Group of European Writers*. Illinois: The Free Press.

SCHNEIDER, D. M. 1961. Introduction: The Distinctive Features of Matrilineal Descent. In D. M. Schneider & K. Gough, *Matrilineal Kinship*. Berkeley: University of California Press.

SELIGMAN, B. 1950. Incest & Exogamy: A Reconsideration. *American Anthropologist* 52: 305-316.

WHITING, J. W. M. [n.d.]. *Totem & Taboo: A Re-Evaluation*. MS. Laboratory of Human Development, Harvard University.

NOTES ON CONTRIBUTORS

BURRIDGE, KENELM OSWALD LANCELOT. Born 1922, Malta; educated at Oxford University, M.A.(Jurisprudence), Diploma in Anthropology, B.Litt.; Scholar with The Australian National University, Ph.D.

Research Fellow, University of Malaya, 1954-56; Asst. Professor, University of Baghdad, 1956-58; Lecturer in Ethnology, Pitt Rivers Museum, Oxford, since 1958.

Author of *Mambu: A Melanesian Millennium*, 1960.

DOUGLAS, MARY. Born 1921, Italy; educated at Oxford University, B.A., B.Sc., D.Phil.

Lecturer in Social Anthropology, Oxford, 1950-51; Lecturer in Anthropology, University College, London, 1951-63; Reader, 1963.

Author of *The Lele of Kasai*, 1963; *Purity and Danger*, 1966.

FOX, ROBIN. Born 1934, England; educated at the London School of Economics and Political Science (University of London), B.Sc.(Sociology), Ph.D.(Anthropology).

Teaching Fellow, Harvard University, 1958-59; Lecturer in Sociology and Social Anthropology, Exeter University, 1959-63; Lecturer in Anthropology, London School of Economics, 1963.

Author of 'Witchcraft and Clanship in Cochiti Therapy', in Ari Kiev (ed.), *Magic, Faith and Healing*, 1964; 'Tory Island', in B. Benedict and T. Smith (eds.), *Problems of Smaller Territories* (in press); *The Keresan Bridge* (in press).

LEACH, EDMUND RONALD. Born 1910, England; educated at Cambridge University, B.A.(Maths. Mechanical Sciences); London University, Ph.D.

Research Officer, Sarawak, 1947; Asst. Lecturer in Anthropology, London School of Economics, 1948; Lecturer, 1949; Reader, 1950; Lecturer in Anthropology, Cambridge University, 1953; Reader, 1958. Fellow of King's College, Cambridge, 1960; Provost, 1966.

Author of *Social and Economic Organization of the Rowanduz Kurds*, 1940; *Social Science Research in Sarawak*, 1950; *Political Systems of Highland Burma*, 1954; *Pul Eliya: a village in Ceylon*, 1961; *Rethinking Anthropology*, 1961.

Editor of *Aspects of Caste in South India, Ceylon and North-West Pakistan*, 1960.

LÉVI-STRAUSS, CLAUDE. Born 1908, Belgium; educated at the University of Paris.

Has held positions at the University of São Paulo, at the New School for Social Research, New York, and at the École Pratique des Hautes Études, Paris. French Cultural Attaché in the United States, 1946-47. At present Professor of Anthropology at the Collège de France, Paris.

Author of *Les Structures élémentaires de la parenté*, 1949; *Tristes Tropiques*, 1955; *Anthropologie structurale*, 1958; *La Pensée sauvage*, 1962; *Le Totémisme aujourd'hui*, 1962; *Mytho-logiques: Le Cru et le cuit*, 1964.

MANN, COLIN NICHOLAS JOCELYN. Born 1942, England. Studied at Cambridge University, B.A. 1964.

Research Fellow of Clare College, Cambridge.

Co-editor of Medieval French Literature section of *Year's Work in Modern Language Studies*, vol. xxvi (1964), 1965.

MENDELSON, E. MICHAEL. Born 1928, France; educated at Cambridge University, B.A.(Hist.; Eng. Lit.), M.A.; University of Paris (Cert. Centre de Formation aux Études Ethnologiques; Élève Titulaire, École des Hautes Études Pratiques); University of Chicago, M.A., Ph.D.

Lecturer in Asian Anthropology, School of Oriental and African Studies, University of London, since January 1960.

WORSLEY, PETER MAURICE. Born 1924, England; studied at Cambridge University, B.A.; Manchester University, M.A. (Econ.); Australian National University, Ph.D.

Research Assistant, Manchester University 1949-51, 1954-55; Lecturer in Sociology, University of Hull, 1956; Senior Lecturer 1951-64; Professor of Sociology, Manchester University, 1964.

Author of *The Trumpet Shall Sound*, 1957; *The Third World*, 1964.

YALMAN, NUR OSMAN. Born 1931, Turkey; studied at Cambridge University, B.A., M.A., Ph.D.

Bye-Fellow of Peterhouse, Cambridge 1956-58; Fellow, Center for Advanced Study in the Behavioral Sciences, 1960; Asst. Professor of Anthropology, University of Chicago, 1964; Assoc. Professor of Anthropology, University of Chicago, 1965.

Author of 'On the Purity of Women in the Castes of Ceylon and Malabar', *Journal of the Royal Anthropological Institute*, 1963; 'Dual Organization in Central Ceylon? or the Goddess on the Tree-top', *Journal of Asian Studies*, 1965, and other papers.

AUTHOR INDEX
AND BIBLIOGRAPHY CROSS-REFERENCE

Details of text references are given in full in short biblio-graphies at the end of each paper. In the listing below, reference to particular titles is indicated by figures in brackets. Thus 'Barbeau, M. (1950: 46)' refers to the item 'Barbeau, M., 1950' fully described at p. 46 of this book.

Index

Lévy-Bruhl, L., 100
Locke, J., 125
Lockwood, D. (1956: 158), 157 n. 5
Long, J. (1791: 139), 129

Macbeath, A. (1952: 158), 157 n. 3
McClelland, D. C. (1951: 178), 172 n. 5, 177 n. 5
Malinowski, B., xvii, 130, 145, 164
  (1927: 178), 171, 177 n. 4
  (1932: 178), 12, 177 n. 4
  (1935: 178), 177 n. 4
Mann, C. N. J., vii, 1, 180
Marrett, R. R., 176 n. 2
Marx, K., xi, xviii, 52, 92-100, 111, 112, 113, 141, 157
Mauss, M., 10, 27, 96, 122, 133; *see also* Durkheim & Mauss
Mendelson, E. Michael, viii, xi, xix, 119-139 *passim*, 126, 180
Miller, H. (1936: 158), 141
Mills, C. Wright (1963: 158), 157 n. 1
Montesquieu, C. L., 96
Murdock, G. P. (1949: 178), 164, 169
Myres, Sir J., 114 n. 2

Nadel, S. F. (1951: 178), 176
  (1954: 158), 157 n. 3
Needham, R. (1962: 69), 58
Neumann, J. von (1958: 139), 138 n. 3

Parsons, T., 157 n. 5, 164
  (1949: 178), 176
Piaget, J., 151
Pilling, A. R., *see* Hart & Pilling
Propp, V. (1958: xix), xvi

Radcliffe-Brown, A. R., 73, 157 n. 2, 162, 164, 176
  (1929: 139), 130
  (1931: 158), 156
  (1951: 139), 132
Richards, J. F. (1914: 47), 25

184